Your Financial Future

How to Manage and Maximise Your Money

IAN LEES

Your Financial Future

First published in 2016 by

Panoma Press Ltd
48 St Vincent Drive, St Albans, Herts, AL1 5SJ, UK
info@panomapress.com
www.panomapress.com

Book design and layout by Neil Coe.

Printed on acid-free paper from managed forests.

ISBN 978-1-784520-90-8

The right of Ian Lees to be identified as the author of this work has been asserted in accordance with sections 77 and 78 of the Copyright, Designs and Patents Act 1988.

A CIP catalogue record for this book is available from the British Library.

This book is available online and in bookstores.

DEDICATION

I would like to dedicate this book to Mrs Janet McDermott, in Jedburgh, without whom I would not be here. My grateful thanks and my best wishes to her family.

ACKNOWLEDGMENTS

My Mum and Dad.

Mr Henry Bell was my first science teacher and head of the Boys' Brigade. He introduced me to the Boys' Brigade and was most rational and inspirational.

Mr Iain Lamont, Head of Law and Accounts, Perth University, who made law (a dry and accurate subject) interesting - together with accounts. He was motivating and taught me to challenge when things did not add up.

Mr Graeme Norvell, Head of Economics, who stirred my interest and started my passion in the subject.

Mr Andy Franchi, who gave me my first real job opportunity in sales, took an interest, guided me, and trained me on how to deal with people, to develop and look after clients' best interests, which would in turn be in my best interests too.

To the many highly qualified members, friends and colleagues of the industry of insurance CII, LIA, PFS, IFS and the IFP from whom I learned so much.

CONTENTS

CHAPTER 1:
Introduction and background

With all the massive advances in medical science, technology and media services, there is a surge towards changes in lifestyles and increased improvements to living standards and to the quality of life, but there is very little financial planning advice for couples in their late thirties and mid to late forties in modern society.

Caught in a difficult period when the wave of baby boomers (babies conceived at the end of the Second World War) and men and women returning home and trying to rebuild their lives and return to normal has been one cause of a wave of people who suddenly required jobs and houses. These consumers were the cause of increased demand from a limited supply. Subsequently a bubble in the market was causing prices to rise as the supply was unable to keep up with demand. This baby boomer bubble produced a ripple effect and those who have made use of the great leaps forward helped to drive up property prices, which has now all but come to an end. Reality and realism has replaced the reckless abandonment of ever-increasing property prices. Banks have allowed this to happen, relaxed their processes, to allow individuals to build up debt, upon which they will profit further.

More recently, the influx of immigrants, due to the removal of barriers by the Labour government, permitted and encouraged an influx of immigrants from many areas in Europe and the Middle East. This has further increased demand to where we now have too many people chasing too few properties and jobs. The housing shortage and subsequent problems have been exacerbated by these events. The labour skills shortage, lack of house building, or utilising uninhabited and redundant land and properties has led to even fewer habitable properties. One reason for this was higher wages in the UK in comparison to some other European countries, so migration for work and higher wages, to be able to send money home, or back to families to improve their lifestyles, is having a further impact on the UK economy and the demand and supply.

Recently with the increased pressures on the immigration policy we have seen a completely new wave of people, many of whom are not skilled, entering the UK, filling basic jobs and reducing the wages for everyone – except the few at the top (Source: *The Economist*). These top executives are involved in the revolving door of employment. We see those at the top moving around in circles from regulator to bank employee or insurance company employee. In many cases these are predators of employment who are continuously on the move – to fill vacant top end employment blackspots – and who are neither leaders nor entrepreneurs but gap fillers, willing to do as they are told rather than provide leadership or quality of management.

In previous centuries, and even more recently in the 1930s, it was unheard of for couples to divorce, or to have extra-marital affairs which, if discovered, the consequences of such dalliances were robustly rebuffed. In those days prior to ladies getting the opportunity to vote, they had little input or engagement in life. Women were chaperoned and could not easily find out what their potential partner was like until after marriage. Similarly neither men nor women could discover and develop their relationship prior to marriage which more often than not had to be agreed with the father or matriarch of the household. An explanation of a suitor's means of income and his intentions towards the potential spouse, his ability to keep the daughter in the lifestyle to which she had become accustomed, and her wellbeing going forward were paramount.

It required a deep and meaningful conversation with the intended family and very often needed nerves of steel.

The opportunity to live together was frowned upon by the churches, communities, families and friends, and tarnished reputations of ladies was sufficient to deter the most amorous of encounters.

Since then, women have had to fight to get their basic rights: the opportunity to vote, their battle for equality, all hampered by their intransigent male counterparts. Their quest continues to be a struggle today. The opportunities for women have come out of their fight for freedom and independence by ladies like Emily Pankhurst, resulting in women having more opportunities than ever before. As a result of this struggle, women have been able to carve out their own careers, generate greater independence for themselves, with many more opportunities and prospects, to the betterment of all.

Equally as a result, men have also had to change and continue to adapt and compromise, which is generally seen as good for all. The structure of family life is so much different from when I was brought up, and the benefits of more social engagement and increased technological interaction means friends and families can be far more removed and spread out geographically. As society increases, and with the current lack of good quality jobs available in the UK, many younger people are looking to Australia, Canada and Europe where they feel they may have many more opportunities. This brings with it many social problems for the country of origin and those taking in new immigrants, causing serious and completely different new social problems.

The use of the internet, Skype and new media contact is available 24 hours a day, seven days a week and time can be set aside to bring people and families together in ways we never thought possible before. Technology is with us, is advancing rapidly and is here to stay. With technology come many more exciting possibilities and with these, areas of concern such as data protection and computer hacking. Everyone must be vigilant and everyone must take much more responsibility for their actions. We are entering a new era in communications where society uses the new 'smart' technology and business will in future be conducted in a completely different manner. As a result, everyone needs to be much more aware of their actions and we must all be more on our guard.

As we move forward into a new era, we can't change the past but we can learn from it. You can use your experiences and the information you learned to apply logic on which you can build and make lasting changes from which you can benefit personally, socially and financially. Using these new technological advances you can build, develop and enjoy the lifestyle you wish.

Reason for this book

The inspiration for this book was brought about as a result of many years as a product-flogging salesman in the industry of insurance. I was then and still am a life assurance salesman – and proud of it.

We were given specific products which required salesmen and women like myself to go out and find enough people to purchase these products. Salespeople (and there were many) were given product training and a product spiel, which required us to go out and play 'the numbers game'. The objective was to sell a sufficient number of products to meet our targets and obtain our commissions in order to live. The old selling requirement was to speak to 30 people a week, make 10 appointments which would result in three product sales a week, for which we were remunerated by insurance company commissions. It still works just as well today as it did then. The job and process was to get the appointment.

What does not happen from this approach is building up a sustainable business for the adviser, or a trusted business relationship for the client, and the volume of business which stayed on the books for insurance companies was fickle and unsustainable. This process does not build up a solid business with an ongoing income stream, or a long-term business strategy of being a trusted adviser with all clients. The real difference between flogging a product where no real business relationship exists and where providing you speak to sufficient numbers of people, and there are enough of them who will purchase a product at least every six years on average, without any commitment by the adviser or product provider or from the client.

I wanted to generate a new model: a profitable, sustainable, ethical and professional business, working with clients over the long term to develop trust and a long-term business relationship.

The changes in social structure, the increasing mortality of men and women, the advances in medical science, the major changes to people's lifestyles and their expectations, led me to challenge my own way of thinking.

As a result of the increasing number of women in the workplace, with more opportunities and available work and the introduction of the 'house husband', there are changes to family dynamics creating a need for the constant monitoring of life, income and expenditure, but also an increase in levels of anxiety and stress. With these changes come less fun, a reduction of pleasure in life, less enjoyment, less meaningful jobs, the extension of work patterns beyond the state retirement age (currently 65 for men and 60 for women but increasing for many due to the lack of funding) and the ever-increasing quest for control and independence. More women are now looking to carve out careers in business for themselves, sometimes becoming the main breadwinner in the family, which can mean taking the decision to have children later in life in order to be able to preserve their desired lifestyle and so delay dealing with the consequences until some time in the future.

In addition to this, for those approaching retirement we have seen the State Pension Scheme(s) crumble due to gross negligence by successive governments and their decisions to defer taking any action. The desire of governments to offload their duties and responsibilities on to future governments, insurance companies and other institutions have all contributed to the failure within the State Pension Scheme and those beneficiaries who have been financially disadvantaged. These people have contributed throughout their lives with the expectation they would receive the State Pension at age 60 and 65 respectively. These pension dates have now been extended. For example, a lady who was expecting to get her pension scheme at 60 has now been notified she will have to wait until age 67. This means the lady has lost seven years' State Pension benefits worth £40,094.60 (i.e. £110.15 per week as a single person x 52 [weeks] x seven [years]). The current State Pension is now £115.95 per week for 2015/2016.

The added opportunities in UK society provide more choice in the type of work, flexible hours and fewer restrictions on daily life. This, along with people choosing to work with their lifestyle at the forefront of family decisions, is why I identified a gap in the market for women and couples in their late thirties and early to late forties to choose the lifestyle they want to achieve and the means by which they could adopt a plan, a process and adapt a strategy to help them realise their objective.

Objective: choose your desired lifestyle

To accomplish this means working out what you want to achieve, when you want to achieve it, and making concessions to help you succeed with your objectives.

Our research found couples now have much greater expectations than ever before. Couples who wish to be considered to be successful want to develop a lifestyle and maintain it, now and in the   future and throughout retirement.

A gap year after university is now perceived as a 'must' before settling down. Financing this gap year along with the lifestyle required means this needs to be revised and updated according to the student's expectations. The breakaway from the old traditional values of the man being the breadwinner and mother staying at home to look after the children has changed dramatically for many more people. I refer to the breadwinner as the 'hunter gatherer'; this can now be either partner, depending on the jobs and/or salaries available. Having children often has a significant influence over family life, type of job and choice of career, and the parents' social interaction is often directly influenced by the children. This change in lifestyle has been complemented with advances in education. Universities allowed women the opportunity of extended learning and social interaction, to take decisions to be more selective, more independent, and more enthusiastic. Sometimes reduced quality of educational establishments means parents need to move, to purchase property in the school postcode and catchment area, which has an impact on the area and increased property prices.

With these changes comes the dramatic effect such moves can have on their family finances. Where planning for insurance for life used to include long-term savings for a future together, the introduction of concern about what may or may not happen introduces an element of fear on protection and savings, and confusion and anxiety over long-term planning. One thing which remains constant is the desire to give their children the best opportunities available. This may mean anything from moving home to contributing to the child's gap year or being there at times of anxiety and stress.

With these massive changes in working practices, more women in the workplace, and growing social changes have all contributed to more and more women becoming much more independent and establishing themselves as the main breadwinner in the family. The man has had to compromise and become the house husband in some instances. Couples are now having in-depth conversations and deciding on the most appropriate use of their knowledge and skills: who has the best skillset and can make the most of the opportunities, to help them be more efficient as a family and to achieve and enjoy the lifestyle they wish.

Given all the changes in social media, the speed of information and the increased volume means it is important to assess the situation more fully. Unfortunately, this also creates uncertainty and the need to ensure the information provided is accurate and up to date.

Sport and recreation have developed and additional opportunities have flourished for both sexes and their children. The balance of careers and individual lifestyles, and much more independence in life, changes to marriage and the introduction of civil partnerships, has introduced much more freedom. Expectations are increased, and the desire to live for the present becomes more attractive.

Sadly, with these increases in freedom we are seeing the breakdown of marriage and civil partnerships. The family separations have increased which means more people are changing their commitment to their partners, bringing with it more complex family arrangements. As a result of these changes, new family structures can mean one family separating and becoming two: additional families with different sets of children from previous marriages. Partners try to retain a family type of unit and family balance to care for each child and family member, their partner and their offspring. These changes in family values and structures play a very significant role in the family finances – now more than ever before.

Changing lifestyles

However, changing lifestyles, work patterns, lack of job security, job sharing and the reduced quality of employment introduces added stress, which means difficult decisions must be made. The areas of concern need to be addressed at the earliest possible opportunity, to retain balance, family security and sometimes your sanity. Having a plan is essential.

Making a plan and developing a strategy has always been at the heart of any success. However, before you can make a plan you need to decide on what you want to achieve. From a personal financial perspective, you need to make a Will upon which you can build your family tree, arrange your finances and prepare for passing wealth down through the family. Knowing who you wish to benefit after your death prepares the basis for your lifestyle planning.

Once this step has been established you are then in a position to develop a plan and set up a process which keeps your strategy flexible, to ensure you can amend your plan as required and you will achieve what you want out of life. Once you put a plan in place it must be in writing, it must be monitored to ensure your aims and objectives have not changed and that you remain on track.

Without a plan or without a goal, you will have no lifestyle strategy. You will bounce around life, flitting from one event to the next, dealing with events and crises on an ad hoc basis as they arise or in some cases after the event. To react repeatedly to events in this way is to lose control. To be in control you need to know what you want and how you intend to get it. One way to relieve the pressure and reduce the stress of this is to develop your lifetime cash flow plan and to set about preparing for unforeseen eventualities. Without a plan there is little or no direction and you end up just reacting to whatever life throws at you. This becomes tiresome, increases confusion and saps your energy.

The Boy Scout motto of 'Be Prepared' is a great motivator into action!

In this book I want you to assess and develop a lifetime cash flow plan to implement a process and strategy to help you take control.

There are no secrets to success.
It is the result of preparation, hard work.

COLIN POWELL

CHAPTER 2:
The fundamentals (back to basics)

Once we are born we have certain specific needs and basic requirements such as water, food, heat, light, and as we develop we see the vast changes in our bodies, our surroundings and our requirements and our need to adapt to the changes in our lifetime. We become more inquisitive, more interested and want more. We become engaged, we become ambitious, our revised expectations and desires mean we want to get more out of life. As someone once said, life is not a rehearsal, you are only here once so make the most of it. To get the best out of life and make the most of it, you have to be more fully involved, but make sure you become involved effectively and efficiently to get the lifestyle you want to live.

During my career of looking after clients' money and financial advice, I have seen some advisers treat their customers with the utmost contempt. Some advisers appear to treat their customers as being stupid, use lots of industry jargon, acronyms, or abbreviations to sell or promote themselves as 'experts' rather than look to engaging and building an ongoing commercial business relationship with their clients. By selling products with hefty levels of commissions available it encourages salespeople to find the clients to fit their product. This deliberately creates a situation which develops an inherent distrust and introduces bias into their recommendations. This also reduces the level of client trust and is certainly due to the techniques used and as a result of these product-flogging advisers. Banks and tied advisers are good examples of this type of ignorant commercialism where there is little or no commitment to customers.

What these product-flogging people are doing is looking after themselves rather than looking after their clients.

Starting out?

Most people start their careers on the basis of advice given at school, through religion, or their families and friends. From the classroom to the working environment we are educated in the basic skills needed and given a general direction. Schools and colleges play a further part in our education and our decision process to qualify for a job, go into an apprenticeship or qualify and develop into our chosen career, such as one of the professions. Each of these establishments provides us with education, expertise and skills in dealing with these areas. The professions with their requirements to attain a certain level of knowledge and the necessity to work in practices for a number of years before being offered a partnership means years of low wages and time spent under professional supervision in their 'apprenticeship'. This process helps trainees in learning their trade, honing skills for their profession, and there is an element of protection due to their practice management and control. Gaining skill and experience through a hands-on approach.

The quality of the information, knowledge and experience gained in these formative years helps us to develop our individual skills.

Knowledge is not just about what you know, it is also about knowing what you don't know.

In these early years it is easy to be effective and efficient, enthusiastic and motivated, driven by ambition to do well. Any deviation or errors will be challenged and changed by parents or teachers. As we reach the age of maturity with the onset of responsibility and eagerness to be a success, the motivation and the eagerness may start to gradually subside to be replaced with repetitive procedures, lack of interest and lethargy. Lethargy is an emotional disease which more importantly can eat into our enjoyment of life and starts a downward spiral. Recognising apathy, realising we may be reducing our effectiveness, and reducing our control over life become a chore. If we become bored with life it shows in our work and in our play.

As our lifestyle wanes, what was perceived as a challenge becomes a chore and if we experience a lack of money, we can start watching others with envy. A lack of money focuses the mind on that specific issue. Others may develop and build their family finances in many ways at difficult times. With these differences can develop greed or the need to 'keep up' when some people seem to be doing so well, perhaps set up home with their partner, start a family, and appear successful with their personal life as well as their work. This may make some people envious when comparing themselves to their peers or colleagues. All these play on our minds and eat away at our confidence.

CASE STUDY

A client of mine went through what he described as his mid-life crisis at 44 years old. He saw friends and colleagues earning reasonable amounts of money, enjoying good holidays and it was brought home to him when his friend purchased a ski chalet in the Alps. He claimed he was tired of life, depressed and emotionally drained. When we drilled down into his life, and his wife's life, he had a high-pressure job, his wife was involved more fully with the local community, and we looked at the children who were in private education. We sat down and calculated their income and expenditure and their cash flow. We examined why the children needed private education, his job, how his wife coped and we looked at the school funding and their outstanding mortgage debt. The build-up of pressure and decision making was taking its toll on the family. He was demotivated and could not see a way out.

After gathering the information we soon realised and identified he was trying to fund everything out of income, his income. By identifying the bigger picture, and after a long and serious discussion, we reached an agreement: we rearranged their mortgage and used their tax-efficient investments to pay for school fees. I pointed out they had been making savings for such an event but had failed to use it. They had forgotten the reason behind making these savings and were reacting to situations. Family outings and events were restricted to being a taxi driver for the children, and/or each other, family meals were disjointed and quick, and events were becoming a chore.

Basically we showed them how they could actually afford to live on their earnings; they could pay school fees out of existing savings, releasing pressure on the need to work, to scrimp and save and pay bills. We also built into their plan an activity holiday with the children (where Mum and Dad had to take part) each year. The next yearly review was so incredibly different, less tense and they also brought in the photos from their activity holiday. This was their family holiday. The only thing they did not do was the children wanted them to do a bungee jump, which mum and dad refused and I could not agree more with their decision!

Life is not about working and earning enough to survive. Life is all about earning, learning and enjoying your family, and your finances, which means making your money work efficiently.

Life assurance salesman

When I first started selling life assurance, I was amazed at the amount of money we advisers could make. However, we did have to earn it. It needed an enthusiastic and very flexible nature and the wherewithal to accept rejection – and lots of it.

When I first started in direct sales, after going through the product training and sales training my first boss took me out to lunch, in his Daimler, to his country club where everyone called him by his surname. This impressed me and demonstrated to me the respect he had earned and he told me that I could get all this if I worked hard. This is known as the carrot and the stick method, feed their greed.

The calculations for success were simple. I had to telephone 30 people per week; I would get 10 appointments and three sales.

Insurance commissions for advisers were 60% of first year's premiums, to reflect the work in finding clients, the sales process and the work involved in 'getting the sale'. We were trained with successful advisers who constantly pestered clients trying to get them to make 'the decision', to get the sale. There are many tricks of the trade to get what was referred to as the 'wet signature' on the contract.

The bottom line was the commissions available. We could generate 60% of first year's premiums for our commission. Some contracts paid 90% which reflected the difficulty in the sale of the type of product. Longer term contracts generated higher levels of commissions, e.g. pensions set to age 75 – the latest selected pension age at that time.

Where I sold an insurance policy for £50 per month I would generate £360 commission for myself. That worked out to be £1,080 per week and 52 weeks in the year – £56,160. My manager told me if I only worked 48 weeks, and took four weeks' holiday, that worked out to be £51,840 per annum in 1979. That was good money to me, a student. I was motivated, I was excited! Then I heard those exciting, uplifting and most motivating words that most salesmen hear from sales managers: "Go get 'em tiger."

Commissions by way of remuneration

Whilst we earned generous commissions of 60% and more, envious journalists failed to inform the reason for the way this commission was designed. If a client purchased a 25-year contract, rather than obtain a small amount of commission under the insurance company, sales agents had a non-indemnity agency contract. Understanding that salespeople could not live on such a meagre amount, and the length of time it would take to get up to any reasonable living wage, they offered an indemnity commission. Secondly, the insurance company would have to provide a loan which would increase their debts and liabilities.

To offset this, the insurance companies introduced indemnity commissions to reward their agents. The insurance companies offered a one-off lump sum commission on the sale of the contract, often not reclaimable if the contract went off the books. To calculate indemnity commission meant the insurance company calculated the commission to be paid over the term on a non-indemnity basis, took their fee, and came up with a figure which would be acceptable to salespeople. These commissions were flexible and differed with each company. The salesperson still obtained a small amount of monthly commission from the original non-indemnity premium to pay for a salesperson to 'service the product and client' over the contract term.

In many instances commission was set around 60%, negotiable from each company, and higher for higher producing insurance company sales agents. In those days a salesperson could only be contracted under law to one insurance company. Hence the one-off lump sum upfront payment with a much lower ongoing commission – usually some 2.5% of the monthly premium. The insurance company offloaded their risk on to their agents, many of whom were self-employed, and often unaccountable to and uncontrolled by the insurance company or their client. Within the contract during the term, the insurance company charged some 1% or more as an annual fee, plus other charges, plus any contract penalties if a contract was terminated before the end of the agreed term.

What my manager omitted to tell me was that based on the results of my sales activity he would receive 20% of my income as my manager, the assistant manager would receive 15% and there was a bonus for the employees on the administration side of my work. All these costs and charges are taken from client contributions.

I do not regret my time in direct sales, in fact I cherish the opportunities it has opened up. It was hard work, it was tedious at times, and it could be cruel and very emotional. The highs were high and the lows could be very low – but I learned some of the most valuable lessons and some of the best skills from my peers. I met and mingled, and learned with some of the best in the industry, the industry giants.

The problem I foresaw was there was no ongoing advice or service for clients. It was purely a numbers game. A salesperson built up a client bank, by whatever means, and sold products as often as they could – for no good reason. The problem was no control from insurance companies – in quality of salesperson, or management, or quality of product sold, or quality of service, or service agreement to the client.

Success comes in many guises though. Each person is motivated in different ways, spurred on by different emotions and various achievements. Some people in management use the carrot and stick method to encourage whilst others can be much more influential, committed and instructive. Whatever method or strategy you choose to use to meet your goals, it is important to have a sound robust process in place: a process and a procedure and the ability to monitor which keeps you in control and helps to drive your enthusiasm, to create opportunities. More importantly, your plan keeps you on track to refer back to it at any stage allowing you to meet your own individual desires and objectives.

A sound strategy and process in place helps you be ahead of the game rather than chasing it.

Success – a world of opportunities

Success means different things to different people. Success can be passing your exam, or passing your driving test or getting your first car. For me passing my driving test first time was a major achievement in my life; it was the culmination of various types of transport in my first 18 years. We lived at Heatheryford tomato farm, three miles outside Kinross.

To go into the nearest town (Kinross) to meet friends or go to the cinema or the preferred meeting place, the fish and chip shop, or to the Boys' Brigade or the Air Training Corps (ATC) meant I had to walk. So I developed a plan. What I needed was a bicycle but I couldn't afford one, so I learned how to build a bicycle, with the help and assistance of my father, from many other less worthy machines. This gave me my freedom. To date this was my success story – it meant I didn't have to walk everywhere. If I could build a bicycle, I could travel faster and further and be less tired. It opened up a whole new world. It could get me to school quicker and best of all leave more time for other things. It also meant I could get a job as a newspaper delivery boy and earn money to save up for other things. I could get a better bike to help me with my paper round or help me get a job with the Co-op as a groceries delivery boy. I had an objective, I had a strategy, and I had a solution – my plan.

By adopting a plan, one thing led to another, and this opened up a whole new world of opportunity. The objective and the strategy were in place, although I didn't know it at the time. Pocket money meant even more options and other opportunities opened up. I discovered then that money is only a means of keeping count.

Meeting people

Success can be meeting the right person or people, enjoying their company, enjoying a certain lifestyle, being a part of a group or becoming a major achiever.

Making money is only a very small part of becoming a success. In my opinion, making money is only a means of keeping count. The process is the way in which we achieve our objectives. The strategy is the way we go about achieving our objectives. We obtain money as a result of work carried out and the trust we develop in our dealings with our customers, which brings with it the reward and remuneration from satisfied customers. With process and strategy comes integrity and trust which builds success. Most of us need to work to make money to keep ourselves in the lifestyle to which we have become accustomed. Money helps you reach your goals and meet your objectives – and money can be used to keep a record of how your life is progressing. Money can also be the reward for meeting your goals and achieving your desires. There is an inherent need for money to allow us to do the things in life we wish to do. Money is only a means, a 'facilitator' for agreeing remuneration for work carried out – whether on a one-off project, or as part of your working week.

Some people may try to circumvent the hard work required. Where hard work is replaced by greed and avarice and cutting corners or cutting out vital areas required, there may appear to be short-term success but it does not have substance. The road to a product sale can be eased by cutting out vital elements: for example, in the information gathering process, a basic client fact find, or driving a sale through using false and misleading claims or statements. Cutting corners or missing vital information means the product may not do the job.

This type of sale is known as 'reverse the hearse up and let them smell the flowers'. Forcing a sale is not the way to engage, or educate, or build trust for a long-term business association.

The banking and insurance industries have demonstrated this greed and avarice, playing the numbers game with their clients, and their client banks. It is shown to be ill–placed, and while it may provide short-term results, it is a scenario for disaster and distrust for their clients immediately and over the medium to longer term. I refer to this type of selling as 'shooting fish in a barrel', where the target is the financial institutions client, who has been targeted for a sale. They scour their client banks, using specific criteria to find a suitable target. Products and client banks, when utilised, are often sold on and client banks targeted by the product provider, e.g. mortgage 'books' (i.e. a product provider's mortgage client bank) of client banks in the nineties, sold for a quick lump sum.

Identifying pockets of money

With more people now living together first and getting married later in life, and more marriages breaking down than at any time in the past, I believe money should be kept separate, on an individual basis. One reason for this is to identify who earned what and when, and secondly for tax efficiency and control.

By adopting this strategy it is so much easier to keep count. Calculating tax, whether Income Tax, Capital Gains Tax, National Insurance etc. can be more easily achieved and opportunities exploited.

Unfortunately most people use money as the be-all and end-all. People tend to use money as the objective, whereas I want to demonstrate throughout this book that money helps you pay for the things you want to achieve out of life, your aspirations and your desires in life, but it is not the end itself. Money is only a means to an end. Money is a facilitator. Money is only a means of keeping count.

Exploiting a profit or gaining access to a tax-free lump sum has many other implications and often complications, such as once you have it, what do you intend to do with it? Many might answer 'spend it', which is good, but it seems rather reckless when the original objective has been achieved yet discarded. A written plan would identify the reason behind the original reasoning and decision-making process, and most importantly the objective.

If the only reason is to make money, and vast amounts of it, that is achievable but at the cost of many other things such as family life, enjoyment and friendships – think of Scrooge in *A Christmas Carol*.

Your personal lifestyle

Before you can realise the lifestyle you want to achieve, you need to assess what you want to achieve. Once you know what you want to achieve you can decide on the best method to achieve your objective. Most importantly, you need to develop the cost versus the expenses. An accurate cash flow model can help you monitor and achieve your objective. A cash flow model financial calculation helps you to discover what your options are and discard those which are unnecessary or unachievable, to help you meet your objectives.

I often use a journey from A to B to explain what the objective is – the process we are going to adopt, and what we need to do along the way. If we are driving from London to Edinburgh, you have choices. You can travel by road, rail, air or sea. There are advantages and disadvantages to each.

For example, you are restricted when you travel by air or sea due to the start of the journey at an airport or a harbour. London may offer a number of potential airports, but the port may not be so readily accessible. Other towns may not have so many options. Similarly with rail travel, there may be a number of locations to start from but as with air and sea there may be no destination with a similar facility, or you may have to make use of another facility to achieve your objective. So we discount air, sea and rail due to the restrictions and loss of control on your travel and you may decide on road. Then roads offer further options: speed and freedom and added control may be the main attractions.

	Advantages Time taken	Disadvantages
Motorway	Speed, direct 8½ hours	May be boring, exhausting Volume of traffic and delays Limited stopping places which are expensive Physically and mentally tiring
A Roads	Not so monotonous Opportunities for sightseeing 18-20 hours	Twisting roads and constant changing gear Getting trapped behind caravans, lorries or tractors – tiring
B Roads	24-48 hours	Requires a vast amount of time and accommodation

A journey is a great example for it is not just about getting from A to B, it is an exercise in emotions, dreams, aspirations, mode of travel, solutions, deciding on the most appropriate method out of a range of options. The reason for driving is to harness one of our most basic instincts: the need for control of independence and freedom. Driving allows you to do what you want to do, when you want to do it and you can stop whenever you wish. The end objective requires you to take decisions and make alterations on how you achieve the best solution.

To complement driving look at the car we drive: the engine size, the colour, the type – is it a saloon, estate, sports? Our choice of car gives a perception and an impression of the image we may wish to convey, or unwillingly convey.

Driving to Perth on the motorway with three and four lanes in places, it was interesting to see lorries and some large vans making full use of the inside lane. Many other drivers were hogging the middle lane, some following each other in the outside lane. Constantly driving in the middle or overtaking lane they must be knocking years off their lives, due in part to the anxiety, pent-up anger and frustration of constantly trying to get ahead. Motorway driving brings out the worst and the best in people. Some drivers are determined to beat their opponent instead of being courteous or generous or understanding that moving in and out of lanes is a game for mugs, and rarely achieves any important function. It may save a few minutes of a journey time, but at what cost to themselves or other road users? Watching the 'smart drivers' following each other in the inside lane, moving more efficiently and more effectively with less stress, allowing each other room to manoeuvre or overtake or just being courteous was a joy and an inspiration.

It brought back to mind my driving test. This was highlighted even more when I sat and passed the Institute of Advanced Motorists (IAM) test, and I remember many of the good points from my initial basic driving test that I had been taught, learned and subsequently ignored or had simply forgotten. For example, when driving you should be aware of everything which is around you, and try to anticipate problems or potential issues. With motorway driving you need to be even more aware; you should regularly check your speed and constant use of your mirrors is essential. The old adage 'check your mirrors' – nearside passenger mirror, interior mirror, driver offside mirror and repeat the process – keeps you aware of what is happening all around you and alerted in advance to improper drivers, or speeding motorists. This allows you to make a decision on the best options for the safety of yourself, your passengers and those all around you, and your vehicle. If you intend to turn left or right, check all your mirrors then signal, check and then make your turn to complete the manoeuver. Such a move is merely courtesy to other road users – letting them know what your intentions are. Mirror, signal, manoeuver.

Being in control

Watching the traffic clogging up the middle and outside lanes, it was clear lorry drivers were being smart: doing a steady speed, driving in unison and moving more quickly than the other two lanes which should be used for overtaking. Lorry drivers were aware of what was happening around them. They knew their Highway Code, they knew their own Code, these lorry drivers were in control, they knew they were in the 'smart lane'.

Another example is a runner on an athletics track with six lanes. The runner on the inside lane may have the emotional advantage of seeing the other five competitors ahead of him and provide enough impetus to make the runner put in that little bit of extra effort, which makes all the difference coming off the first bend.

I remember watching the 4 x 200 metres baton relay when the US were dominating the sport and known as the Dream Team. On paper they looked as though they just needed to turn up: big names, fastest times, all gold medal winners in their individual events. This was a team to fear in competition and they knew it. The UK team could have been forgiven for being overawed.

However, rather than focus on the US Dream Team or the potential for losing, the UK team strategy was to send their slowest runner out first up against the best the Americans had to offer, their fastest runner, to do his best. The psychological effect on the UK team when their slowest runner kept up with the Americans' best was immense. In terms of being inspirations I love watching old re-runs and the power of the tactics of our UK team and their great win… and they won in style. Giving the UK team runners such a challenge was inspired, and as a result the Americans appeared to be less focused, they lost their psychological and physical advantage and our UK team, our 4 x 200 metre relay team, won their gold medal. They took a risk, it worked, and they were so successful they have become legends. As an audience we were able to share in their success. Their success was down to good leadership, great tactics, focus and a team for whom winning was the only option.

Had they followed their own natural strategy and instincts, they might have come second as expected. They changed, they adapted, they adopted a new strategy; it was successful, they are now set down in the history of athletics.

New ideas, new solutions.

If you always do what you've always done you'll always get what you've always got.

HENRY FORD (1863-1947)

Life in the smart lane means you start now, you check your current situation as your starting point, you make yourself aware of what you want to achieve. What is available? How you are going to achieve it?

To reach your goal how much risk are you willing to take? Couples and partners need to work together and to check the amount of risk each individual partner is willing to take.

What is risk?

Risk is about taking a chance, taking a gamble. How much risk depends on each individual. There are many types of risks we take on a daily basis: going by car or flying, going by rail or sea. The risks we take can provide great opportunities, by examining the objective, analysing the risk, analysing the worst case scenario and asking yourself can you afford to lose. If so, how much?

In matters financial, as in other aspects of life, each partner will have a different attitude to the amount of risk they are willing to take, or able to take. Risk is not about beating the system or taking a risk for a huge gain. Risk is not about out–thinking someone and not about how fast you make money.

Risk is about setting your objectives, deciding on the length of term, and your experience during the journey. Some people are willing to take high risk. Some people do not want to experience the ups and downs of an investment. Some people do not understand the inherent risk involved in a deposit account.

Different types of asset classes offer different levels of risk and with this, different returns. Risk is all around us in everything we do.

Why take risk?

Couples endure Saturday evening dinners with their in-laws in exchange for a Saturday afternoon of uninterrupted football or rugby or some other activity. Nowadays, few children will pass up the opportunity of watching television or playing on their computers to vacuum the house or clean the car or wash the dishes in return for pocket money. Parents may extend Friday night curfews in return for good behaviour or planned help during the week. Opportunities for sleepovers and other group activities may be used to determine the required parental outcome by such bribery and trade-offs.

Life, like investing, is about trade-offs. The investment trade-off is between the risk and the return. To obtain the return on your investment you require may mean a willingness to accept a different level of risk, at least to some extent.

There are four basic asset classes as follows:

1. Cash

2. Property

3. Gilts, Bonds and Fixed Interest

4. Equities

Within each of these asset classes there are sub-classes.

Each asset class has different properties, various advantages and disadvantages and reacts differently in various market conditions.

Cash accounts and deposit accounts have an inherent risk: the risk of loss of purchasing power i.e. capital loss due to inflation, bank charges etc. Many people view deposit accounts to have no risk, but in reality they do contain risk! Deposit accounts now more than ever before run the risk that the bank or building society may be insolvent or go bankrupt. Bank charges are ever more complex, confusing and increasing. Many basic accounts are increasingly being switched into other less advantageous accounts, e.g. Nationwide, Santander etc. Another risk is the risk of lower returns over the term. Alternatively, the bank may tie you in to a good interest rate now on the basis that inflation will erode that return in their favour rather than the customer's over the term of the contract.

Lower returns are affected by the impact of inflation on the returns. This is known as 'The Real Value of your Money'. This is better described as the purchasing power of your money. Can you remember the lowest amount of money you first paid for fish and chips?

Date   Cost £ _____

Date   Cost now? £_____

Assessing risk in investments is the amount of volatility you are willing to accept for the prospect of, or the opportunity of, a higher return. How much money are you willing to risk? How much are you willing to see your savings and investments go down before it will trigger action? What is your capacity for loss?

Some questions to ask yourself are:

	Financial £	Percentage %
How much of a loss are you willing to accept each year?		
How much can you afford to lose?		
How much can you afford to lose over a five-year period?		
How much risk can you accept from individual investments?		
How do you plan to diversify your various investment risks (market risk, company specific risk, currency risk, economic risk, inflation risk and/or country risk)?		
What risk-related test will an investment have to pass to be held in your portfolio?		
Do you need to accept a higher level of risk to meet your goal?		
When will you need access to your money?		
Will you need access to income during the term?		

Do you need to take a risk or is there a different solution?		
How do you intend to identify the risks involved in your investment?		
How often do you intend to review your investment? Why?		

Banks and insurance company advisers

In the past banks and their tied advisers would select default funds such as 'with profits', or a unit-linked 'managed fund'. Their documents were designed to ensure a higher percentage of clients would confirm their acceptance of their product and their fund by default. Little or no account was taken of the inherent risk through the acceptance of choice of their default fund. It is most unlikely the bank adviser will assess your requirements for comprehensive financial planning. The tied agent for the product provider continues to play the numbers game – for their results rather than the best outcomes for their client.

For example, when I was a broker consultant at Scottish Widows they sold their unit-linked Investor Policy as a 'balanced fund'. Unfortunately, due to lack of transparency and lack of openness, the assets within the fund were not completely disclosed, or the level of risk attaching to this contract. It appears the Scottish Widows management at the highest levels were unaware of the inherent risk to their clients, and their agents sold these products in the absence of knowledge or competence. The directors of Scottish Widows should have been aware, or may be considered to be involved in skulduggery, or a scam. The regulators did discover the inherent risks and misleading advertising on closer inspection, which turned out to be a basket of international shares which included currency risk, country risk, hedging and various other inappropriate holdings. Over and above this, the minimum premium being £10 and costs involved as a result of charges levied was a drag on their clients' investment returns. The charges reflected the amount of work involved in the fund, which was not explained to the customers. It was not made clear the premium of £10 after charges would offer little by way of returns. Put simply, the investor policy had a significantly higher risk than explained in their literature or to clients.

Banks would usually be selling their customers a 'balanced' fund or a 'with profits' fund, both designed to remove one of the most essential areas of investing for and on behalf of customers, taking account of their affordability, the suitability of the contract and the affordability of the contract. The client's profile and their attitude to taking risk is an area which is most time-consuming but essential in order to establish the required return to meet their objectives. One reason behind this strategy is speed and efficiency of the bank or tied adviser to complete their sales process by processing the maximum number of customers in the minimum length of time to maximise their personal commissions and to meet their targets. By cutting corners in this way means: less time is spent with the client, the removal of the client's attitude to taking risk, benefits the bank and bank employees, enables flogging a product with minimal effort and increased commissions for the bank and the employee – at the expense of their targeted customer. Put simply, a poor understanding of their client and poor quality of advice by their restricted adviser. These are considered to be the restricted advisers for the mass market. This is the 'pile them high, sell them cheap' brigade.

Bank salespeople and tied financial advisers would look to select your level of risk on a joint basis, usually on a sliding scale between 1 and 10. The objective was to draw a line then ask their client a closed question, then for a confirmation, and answer of "that will be a balanced fund then" from their salesperson. Such a graph or understanding of your willingness to take risk on the basis of between 1 and 10, or any other scenario, is an exceedingly dangerous lack of understanding for clients and adviser. From a psychological point of view, most clients select the middle i.e. 5 on a scale of 1 to 10, or 50 on a scale of 0 to 100. Try it yourself on a risk scale of 1 to 10 – where would you see yourself? These sales practices replace any proper discussion or interaction with you, the strategy is designed with an end in mind: to select a managed fund and type up their reasons from a template designed for their choice. These sales processes take control away from you.

The sale of these products in this way, the lack of reason for the product terms and conditions, and the lack of explanation are some of the reasons so many policies are terminated by clients in the early years. Such a lack of understanding by a client, and with further losses to the customer through penalties and termination charges, makes much greater profits for the insurance company and removes the liability. The recent ABI (The Association of British Insurers) statistics show that whole of life policies designed to protect the client for the whole of their life are often called 'comprehensive' and have an average term of six years. The whole of life policy is more expensive as a result of inherent risk and because once the contract is established it can run for the client's entire life. It could be used to cover a mortgage in the early years, it could provide for family protection, or business protection, or lifetime protection in many areas. The whole of life policy can protect the cost of school fees or educational fees or it can be used in conjunction with Inheritance Tax planning and building up a tax-free inheritance for children.

Costs of a product – the premium

How much can you afford? How much are you willing to pay? Or is it, how much can an adviser get away with premium wise? One reason for this, as I have explained, is commissions are a percentage of the premium, e.g. 60% of the first year's premium.

Overselling continues to be a major uncontrolled issue. Insurance companies and banks do not complete any checks and are willing to overlook reckless behaviour, profiteering by their salesperson, deceit or fraud, e.g. Libor rigging, pension mis-selling, endowment mis-selling, PPI etc. As a general rule most people opt for the centre or just above or around the middle of the sales pitch. For example, a sales pitch which starts at £20 up to £100 will be around £60. The client settles for the middle and the salesperson confirms that will be £60, which is more often than not accepted. To increase the cost, a salesperson will choose between £50 and £200 – so that will be a premium of £130 then? Your adviser will then provide a written confirmation of 'your choice' along with his reason for your choice. Unfortunately, this is nothing more than a sales pitch and it works in the same way for the premium or amount of money a salesman wants to obtain.

The Contract

The premium and type of contract chosen on a whole of life policy can provide a moving feast for salespeople. For the same amount of premium, the life assurance amount can be manipulated at the expense of investment and, most importantly, the prospects of higher premiums in later life and lower investment returns or significantly lower life assurance, which often defeats the purpose and reason behind the contract.

By looking to provide the appropriate level of protection under a whole of life policy, the sums assured can be manipulated, as can the premium, which will have an effect on your investment returns. Less sums assured, more investment returns. More life assurance required, with lower premiums, means lower investment returns and probably higher premiums later in life.

So many options mean more confusion and anxiety.

There are generally three items which make up a life assurance policy:

- The cost of purchasing the life assurance protection – the premium

- The charges being levied (including commissions)

- The investment content

The older you are at commencement of the policy, the higher the premiums will be. This is called Mortality risk. This risk is due to the risk of premature death for the insurance company, and their view of the risk of having to pay out. The more items or add-ons you build into your contract, the more profitable it may be for the product provider, and you need to take responsibility and weigh up the advantages and disadvantages.

Insurance companies spread risk through third party insurers to reduce their liability.

If you take your decision based on precisely what you require, e.g. protection, savings or pension planning, what benefits you require, your contract terms, etc., your choices become less and your decision made easier. By adopting this strategy you are more easily able to compare contracts for price, quality, service and a good record of paying out claims. Check with the ABI on the quality of claims handling of a company chosen.

CHAPTER 3:
Ian's philosophy on money

Following my success in building a bicycle, gaining independence and harnessing the power of this machine, I was able to get out and about, and earn pocket money which meant I could now afford luxury goods, in my case a pair of real leather football boots. The purchase of football boots meant I might be picked to play in my school football team, or play for a local team. I was able to train mid-week and play at weekends. I now had the transport, and provided I looked after it by cleaning it, oiling it, servicing it and keeping it maintained, it should not let me down. I was rich. I had become independent, I now had control over my destiny – my life had been transformed!

Saving and spending has always been a great part of my life, often spending more than I had earned. From an early age I managed to get a job earning money to enjoy the lifestyle I desired at the time. Money was now my means of keeping count. If I wanted anything I already knew I had to work for it. If I wanted something I had to save up and put simply – *earn it*. That taught me a most valuable lesson in life, the lesson of compromise, the lesson to prioritise and to decide on the most important thing. I had learned from an early age if you wanted something you had to prioritise. I was also taught from an early age you do not borrow money if you want something, you make it an objective, decide on a strategy and work for it.

I was lucky I was brought up to learn to save. We were not well off financially as a family, and my mother and father were always trying to help. There is nothing they would not do to make sure we wanted for nothing. My father worked long hard hours and was the breadwinner in our house. They did not have much money for extravagances. I now had a paper round in the morning and in the evening. During my paper deliveries I managed to get a job as delivery boy at the Co-op two nights a week and earned my first company vehicle: the Co-op bicycle. The Co-op bike was the envy of others because it offered a regular job, pocket money and a place in the structure of the Co-operative Society. This was a heavy metal bicycle with a normal sized rear wheel but with an extra wide tyre, and a smaller wheel on the front, also with an extra wide tyre, to support a huge metal basket frame on the front. A heavy metal frame, one gear and a hard leather, unforgiving saddle which had been out in all weathers – I very quickly learned to make decisions without the benefit of a sat nav to find the quickest and easiest way between two or more points. From the shop to the customer by the least wearisome route i.e. avoiding hills.

It was possible to fit with ease three boxes full of customers' groceries to be delivered in the basket – more or less doubling the weight, and having only one gear such a weight meant it also had the effect of building up my thigh and leg muscles and a dogged determination. This in turn aided my fitness regime and helped with external training for our football team.

One lesson I learned quickly was to get the bicycle up to speed and get to the address at the highest point first – it was downhill deliveries from there. Now that was a plan!

From the proceeds of my diligence and hard work, the following summer during school holidays I persuaded my father to give me a job at Heatheryford tomato farm where we had moved so he could take up his job as manager. I was taken on to do odd jobs, and to fill in when employees were absent, which was often and generally without notice.

I was given the job to fill the large hoppers with anthracite coal. These hoppers were used to feed the great fires from which heat was generated through the water, along large greedy radiators which gave out warmth and protection from cold days and frosts, to help protect and promote growth and redness in the tomatoes. All this away from the chill winds and cold weather of a windy, open, flat, central Scotland. There were 80 greenhouses and one cucumber house; each hopper fuelled a steam boiler which served five of the greenhouses. The hoppers took some two hours of constant, repetitive, heavy work.

My uncle was a manager for the Royal Bank of Scotland at the time and each time he visited he kept trying to persuade me to put my savings in his bank. I had a Post Office account and was saving at a regular rate. The Post Office was simple, local and I understood how it worked. I like to know how things work, it gives me confidence and builds my trust. More importantly, I had easy access to my post office and my account. The nearest Royal Bank of Scotland, the Clydesdale Bank and the Bank of Scotland were all in Kinross and had large imposing buildings, and built up fear and trepidation before entry. They all looked very official and there was an imposing inherent fear which made me feel inferior – which is what they are designed to do. Deposits in the bank belong to them in return for a rate of interest. Once in the bank I would lose my control. Once in the bank would I ever get my money back? I felt intimidated in the bank, they took decisions out of my hands, they told me what was best for me instead of asking me what I wanted.

I later developed that same trait under training in direct sales to earn my commission. Telling people what is best for them is not in my opinion the best way to make friends and influence them, or retain them.

Having an objective, setting up procedures and developing a strategy, putting in place a process has become a way of life with me. It was unintentional at first, but it works. For me, earning money is only a means of keeping count. Keeping an account of the money made demonstrates the success or otherwise of a project. My income stream grew: I received tips for delivering newspapers on time, in good condition, without fail, and for delivering heavy boxes of groceries, for a job well done.

Making money allows me to do the kind of things I want to do – and I have found most other people are of a similar mind. For me it is developing the lifestyle I want to achieve using my skill and knowledge and making judgment calls. I have made errors, many errors, and misplaced judgments but I find it is worth drawing a line under my error or errors; regroup, reassess and move on. Aiming for an objective can be as much fun as achieving it – whether it is a Lamborghini sports car, a new house, designer clothes, a holiday home in the sun, a celebrity cruise or an autumn break in Barcelona. Whatever lifestyle means to you, would you want to give up your lifestyle now, or when you retire at 65 or 75 or 85?

If your lifestyle is to be maintained it has to be planned, cherished and protected – however it also has to be earned. With this in mind you need to prioritise, compromise and implement your strategy.

To enjoy the lifestyle you want, you need to put money aside now as you earn. You need to develop a culture of saving. You need to plan and save for the short term, and save and invest for the medium term, and plan to invest for the longer term. Long-term investments require a different asset class with better opportunities for growth. If you do not engage in a culture of saving and investing you will remain inactive and reacting to events – often using credit cards and costly bank overdrafts. Please be advised banks want you to get into debt, as it is more profitable for them and expensive for you – in charges, interest and one-off amounts for letters and, in the worst case scenarios, debt collection agencies.

Different types of products are required for each event, and for each term: for the short-term cash and yearly interest term deposits and for later life 65 and older income generating products. Growth and income products which include assets which are designed for medium to long-term growth are required for retirement planning. In the medium term you may need money for educational needs such as school fees and university fees, or for buying a larger house to accommodate children for the next 15 to 20 years, before they go off and buy their own property. You may wish to change your car or buy a second car, or require large repairs on your residential property.

It is interesting when I discuss property investments with people as their Personal Financial Planning Coach that when calculating their cash flow they look amazed when I ask them "How much have you set aside for property repairs?" The answer is "Nothing."

When I ask them about their new car, or second car, for the benefit of their cash flow, "How much is the car insurance? What is the cost of servicing? How often does it require servicing? How much does a tyre cost?" The answer is generally they have no idea and as a result have not built this cost into their plan.

I personally find this attitude at best bizarre, at worst ruinous. There is a word for this type of person, in fact I looked it up in the *Oxford English Dictionary* and found four words! Unfortunately, this has an impact on other areas of your finance, your increased costs and charges, and further profits for banks and insurance companies, their directors and their employees.

What is your desired lifestyle?

To develop your desired lifestyle, the advantage of having sufficient money develops control, flexibility, choice and peace of mind.

Money is such an emotive subject it brings with it a wide range of emotions, from quality of life, to envy, greed and criminal offences. With these emotions come more astute savers, to those who will attempt various levels of deceit to criminal offences for they are looking for a quick buck with the willingness to act in the most selfish, self-centred manner, without thought or care on the impact on others around them.

Usually, it may be at a time of death when the estate of a parent is being distributed and families fall out over cash or many other items, even of small or minimal value.

Greed arises in everyone and displays itself in many ways. One example of this is hotels where a room is paid for which includes toiletries in small containers. The guest believes they have paid for these and so they are taken. Hotels lose towels, robes and other items provided for their guests' convenience. It never fails to amaze me why anyone would wish to take the coffee or tea bags or a small plastic bottle of shampoo which reflects around a teaspoonful of shampoo for which a whole bottle can be purchased at Poundworld for 99 pence! Their defensive claim might be it is not stealing because they have paid for it in the price of their bedroom. My point is, why bother? Are they in such financial difficulties that taking a teabag or hotel shampoo will make such a difference to their life? Such an act does *not* improve your life. These people are not beating the system, nor are they making the system better for themselves or anyone else. This is becoming a feature of life, which can only increase the costs of hotel rooms for everyone.

When money becomes involved it alerts others to act and react differently. We can become envious of others, for example between brothers or sisters, which reminds me of the *Bible* and the story of *The Prodigal Son*.

CASE STUDY

One case I recall was of two boys whose father had died some years earlier and their mother passed away without making a Will and it was up to the family, the two boys and their uncle as executors, to distribute the estate.

Unfortunately, the uncle left the boys to get on with it. Mostly it went well until nearing the end preparing for probate when a number of the mother's rings and other significant jewellery went missing. The incident split the family. The two boys did not speak to each other for many years. To add to the distress the younger brother had an old Mini which he had arrived in, and was returning to the army in Germany, so he let his uncle keep the Mini on the basis he would use it on his visits until he returned to England permanently.

For a few years the uncle kept the car, ran it and had it repaired regularly and each year put it through its MOT. But with an ageing car, mounting repair costs and an MOT coming up, the uncle balanced the costs and decided to trade in the old Mini and purchase a nice new Mini. The garage traded in the old Mini as part exchange but it had no real value. The uncle ran the new car for some 18 months and when he died he left his estate to the same two brothers as he had no family. They had looked after him in earlier years, he was part of the extended family, including him in their family outings and meals. In his Will he left the brothers his estate to be divided equally. As executors once again, they had carried out probate and agreed the division of the estate, which was tense but worked through. They had left the Mini to last and the elder brother announced that they should sell the Mini and split the proceeds fifty-fifty but the younger brother claimed the car for himself on the basis the Mini belonged to him as he had lent the original car to his uncle. His argument was the original car belonged to him and he believed that the uncle had replaced the car for a newer model which now belonged to him. Once again this split the family.

The point here was such are the implications of their actions, which had not been thought through. Nothing was in writing and there was no general agreement. Both brothers had different views, which had not been thought through or talked through. Much hostility is introduced into families in this way.

The younger brother's claim on the car brought annoyance, grief and a great deal of hassle to the brothers and drove a massive wedge through their relationship and friendship.

There are many issues and discontent in such matters and, with this in mind, and especially when someone passes away, I believe it is essential that everyone should make a Will. By writing down your wishes it means you control who should get your estate, and in the appropriate amounts which you wish to leave. A valid Will provides clarity, a clear instruction and brings with it peace of mind.

The sales and marketing of insurance products

With banks, building societies, insurance companies and other financial institutions, their inclusion of salespeople paid largely by commissions and targeting their clients is not selling; it is often referred to as 'shooting fish in a barrel'. Insurance companies and banks pay millions to sales and marketing companies to design sales pitches to flog their company's limited range of products rather than put in place any serious or proper financial plan or a strategy for the benefit of their customer.

Banks, insurance companies and advisers who discover their customer has just inherited a large sum or received a large amount of money are targeted by the bank and bank employee apprentices for their one-off product-flogging hit. The maximum commission for the least amount of work, at a time of a client's high emotion. Direct sales people were trained and are still trained to 'hunt' for bank or insurance company clients to exploit: those who have not already been targeted and plundered by the banks' advisers, but external and authorised direct sales people have to find their own clients. These salespeople are often referred to as 'hunters' and less complimentary as 'they eat what they kill'. Once again, it is the 'one-hit' salesmen and women who are targeting opportunities for themselves rather than providing the opportunities for delivering long-term effective and efficient service and financial planning for their clients.

These salespeople are motivated and encouraged by team building and other less attractive processes. They are remunerated by their employer, using the carrot and stick method, and have targets to meet which are often unrealistic, unsustainable and require seriously large volumes of sales to compensate for their more reckless tactics and sales strategies. These product providers sell the type of business their employer needs to sell, e.g. Equitable Life target their products accordingly, flogging with–profits policies in life and pensions to meet their needs, whilst insolvent. Instead of considering the interests of their clients, their old sales activities included flogging pensions with guaranteed annuity rates of up to 20%. History and facts now released show this had not been properly considered by Equitable Life, nor the financial consequences on clients, nor the ramifications on their company when it went wrong, nor the impact this has had on the industry. Insurance companies claimed they would band together to ensure clients would not lose out financially – and after some 20 years' financial redress remains outstanding. The commissions are taken directly from the products by way of charges upfront and in annual management charges, along with a raft of other charges and a regular audit, either a monthly or annual management fee throughout the contract term, and are held within the company and within with–profit funds.

These charges have a dramatic impact on the drag on the investment returns – and more especially if taken from any tax-efficient wrapper. Rather than provide a professional and ethical service, these institutions aim to target and exploit their client banks and fail to provide a strategy or proper process or due diligence to meet customer requirements. Totally Independent Financial Advisers and trusted financial planners offer services to protect their customers with contracts from those inappropriate and unsuitable contracts from the whole of the market, and offer the opportunity to pay by way of open and transparent fees or commission offset in financial terms rather than commissions based on percentages or a mix of both.

Are you a client or a customer?

For the benefit of accuracy I feel it is important to identify the differences in becoming a client or a customer.

Client – a client is someone for whom an adviser has a transactional arrangement.

Customer – is someone who knows what they want and may require a transactional arrangement.

Unfortunately, the industry of insurance and banks sees clients and customers as being one and the same. Insurance advisers, insurance companies and banks 'work their client banks' on the basis of the 80/20 rule, thereby obtaining 80% of their sales from 20% of their client bank. This is the numbers game which continues today. Flogging their products requires 'classification' of their clients/ customers and the further segregation and separation of their clients – to flog their products. More recently we have seen companies and their client banks sold under the claims of 'consolidation' or 'economies of scale'. We need to identify how these benefit the client/customer.

Consolidation is where many products and funds are rolled into one. By consolidating your products or funds you should have a much larger fund as a result, which may attract lower charges as a result of economies of scale. However, you must be clear between consolidation of products and funds and 'churning' of products and funds. Churning is the organised and systematic sales and purchases of funds or products by the salesperson to generate their commissions. Churning is carried out just to increase commissions and charges. It does nothing to enhance or provide trust.

With financial institutions' classification comes segregation and separation of client and service. As a consequence they continue to be 'peddlers' of products and their restricted services.

I believe clients and customers need to be treated like human beings, their goals and aspirations taken into account. Financial planners and advisers need to treat their customers as highly sophisticated, knowledgeable people. Access to information through the internet has created a wealth of people who are much more knowledgeable now than ever before. Checks can be made on advisers and firms, and products and services.

Our objective with our clients is to provide a high-quality comprehensive service and outsource to competent and better qualified people in areas where they can add value.

Working with your financial planner should assist you to agree your adviser's remuneration immediately and upfront. Together you need to set your objectives and design your financial plan accordingly. By working out your income and expenditure and using the correct assumptions, you will develop your lifetime cash flow projection to ensure your income does not exceed your outgoings at any time during your life. By identifying your objectives and your priorities you can have the peace of mind to know what you can afford. By compromise and discussion your requirements can be tailored so they will be achieved now and in the future.

One of the most sensible methods is to put money aside regularly in the right savings and investment products. Safe easy access savings can be achieved with a bank deposit account or Post Office savings account where access to your cash should be instant and available on demand.

Ignore accounts which have restrictions on them, e.g. a VISA card, or unhelpful employees who are determined to refuse you access to your own cash.

It is important to look to what you require from the product and select your account accordingly. Being prepared, instead of going 'rate chasing' and constantly having to move your money. The time spent checking rates, contract terms and finding the most appropriate account takes time and effort. Such time costs are expensive. I remember working in St Andrews as broker consultant for Scottish Widows. On the last Friday of the month there would be queues outside the branch of the building society which had been quoted in the press as having the best interest rate. In those days it only took around 45 minutes to open an account. If they went for a cup of tea or coffee it would probably wipe out any additional savings in interest rates!

The time spent checking rates looking for that extra little percentage was never included in the cost. The savings and costs involved in switching, it is highly unlikely these costs were included. How many people do you know who purchased their family home? They can tell you what it's worth now (or at any time) but it is unlikely they will have deducted the additional costs of estate agents' fees, solicitors' fees, stamp duty or the costs of repairs or new kitchens, which when added together give the true cost of their home. During my career as a tied agent, broker, consultant and Independent Financial Adviser I have never met anyone who can tell me how much interest they have paid their lender – even when mortgage rates were at 16-17%.

It is essential to keep count of all the costs involved as this gives the opportunity to calculate the total real rate of return on your investment. Ask your mortgage lender how much interest you have paid to date and how much they expect you to pay these commercial money lenders. You will be surprised.

CASE STUDY

One client was saving in a Nationwide cheque account because they claimed it offered instant access. When the client wanted instant access he was denied access to his own cash. Nationwide refused to allow the customer to withdraw £2,000 from his £6,000 savings in this Nationwide Instant Access Flexi Account. Then the Nationwide manager terminated the client's VISA card, which is required to withdraw or obtain cash. The client discovered Nationwide advertise a facility to withdraw £500 per day on production of a passport and cheque book. When he produced a cheque book and passport, Nationwide refused to pay out his cash on the basis Nationwide does not recognise the passport as being any accurate form of identity. The chief executive Graeme Beale and chairman Geoffrey Howe refused to apologise, correspond or provide instant access. This meant that the customer was left without cash and could not pay his tradesmen, which meant the tradesmen downed tools and additional delays were experienced whilst other tradesmen had to be found to complete the job.

The customer had to find a financial institution that offered a proper instant access cash facility in the absence of any simple or proper service by Nationwide. By being seriously misled by Nationwide he withdrew the remaining £4,000 and terminated his account – a result of shoddy banking with Nationwide – and moved elsewhere to another institution that provided a better service with trained employees who wanted to help customers.

Be aware of your needs

The lessons to be learned here are to decide on your needs first and foremost and prior to purchasing a product or service. You need to identify your requirements, the type of benefits you may need from this product and build this into your plan.

Beware of incentivised sales or overly friendly salespeople in financial institutions who sell their employers' products for their own benefit i.e. commission and their employers' purposes rather than for the client's benefit.

Take control of your finances

One area that has been at the forefront of my career is budgeting. It is such a simple exercise but it plays the most significant part in your life. It can be boring but any lack of monitoring can lead to mistakes or errors and omissions which may be hard to correct later. The use of call centres for administration and the outsourcing of services to India and the Far East means loss of control of your own finances.

We learn to budget and prioritise what we want from an early age when we are children and given pocket money, and the responsibilities which go with it to help us to decide what we want to do with our money: save or spend. If we spend it, we cannot spend it again and as a result we learn to prioritise and give thought to what we want to achieve. Unfortunately, with the relaxation of banking regulations, the more immoral commercial lenders coax and lure people into debt with their advertising and demonstrations to live for the present and to spend, spend, spend – as long as it is on their credit card, and their advertising does not explain the financial consequences of such actions. Put simply, where consumers have been seduced by the glitter ball of advertising, when the true costs become known, this then becomes a burden because the consumers have to take responsibility for their own actions.

There are many instances where consumers have become entangled in the complex interest rates and fee charges applied by banks and their subsidiaries and partners. Banks and building societies are money lenders – that is what they do. They charge interest at huge rates, and it is in their best interests and to their benefit that you get further into debt, for whatever reason, because the interest and the charges they earn will rack up. It is important to remember these financial institutions are commercial money lenders not philanthropists. In my opinion, anyone who thinks they can beat their bank is sadly mistaken, or a fool. To qualify this statement, please look at the money thrown at advertising. Look at the fortunes commercial lenders pay to highly qualified employees with highly qualified degrees in mathematics and economics and marketing and the volume of people within each bank who control your money. It may be that you only need to miss something by one day to find further charges or loss of interest. Each of these added together makes up the profits of these commercial lenders. This is one reason a bank will offer a client 0.5% interest for depositing money and offer a mortgage loan to another client at an interest rate of some 5% or higher depending on the risk, as a commercial lender, making their turn on your money.

This style of commercial lending, of accessing your money and making some 4.5% interest, and further charging you a monthly premium to have a bank account, is something which needs to be addressed.

Now with the advent of internet peer-to-peer lending becoming more popular and companies like Zoppa bringing people together, it may be possible to obtain a more reasonable rate of interest on your money as they lend out your money to others. It is important to check if this is of financial benefit to you.

It is important to remember these banks employ extremely clever people, and they have invested heavily in highly qualified people, technology and equipment and they are in it for the long term, whilst most depositors tend to only look at their short-term requirements.

The lure of the brand and image

In life and with a family it is around this time when one parent has given up work and two salaries have reduced to one. Children see their friends with all kinds of gadgets and gizmos where the brand name is exploited. Children's egos play on the emotions of their parents and they require a brand name in, for example, a training shoe rather than one from a supermarket.

Those with children see the invasion of repeated sales adverts on television, phones and in the newspapers and events such as Easter and Christmas become one big commercial selling stint which now starts around September.

One of the great opportunities I had was being invited to join Round Table. Round Table is a group of men between 18 and 45. They are usually men in management with similar ideals and want to help in raising money for their community whilst learning new skills and interacting with others from different jobs, backgrounds and viewpoints. We used to run a Christmas float with a Santa going round the houses; we were 'Santa's little elves' collecting as Santa's little helpers and providing local charities with contributions and delivering food parcels to the elderly and the needy.

Those in St Albans and other UK Round Table hotspots knew Christmas was near when the Round Table float manned by volunteers came round. Our thanks go out to those who gave generously, and the enjoyment we had doing this was enormous. One of the great benefits was getting together and helping others from our community, and bringing together many people and organisations and assisting when required. The brand of the Round Table still generates the image of young men helping out, bringing their hard-earned cash to good quality charitable organisations. There are many other good quality organisations such as Lions Rotary who conduct similar operations for the benefit of their community.

Each of these are great training grounds and learning experiences in life – goodwill and opportunities to engage and develop. Like your finances, getting involved is crucial to success.

CHAPTER 4:
We cannot change the past

Helping you facilitate what you want to achieve

We have all made decisions in the past we may regret, and with the benefit of hindsight we might have made a different call – but we can't change the past.

We can, however, learn from it. We can build on our experiences and learn from the experiences of others.

We live in an ever-changing society and finance changes quicker than almost any other area. We need to keep up to date with changes in legislation, changes in banking laws, changes in tax, changes in products, sales and marketing ploys, sales strategies and techniques from highly sophisticated companies with money to splash.

We live in ever-changing times and flash new products, sometimes overpriced or oversold or inappropriately sold, sometimes to unsuspecting customers, means we need to remain ever vigilant. A cynical person might look to the reason behind the sale and who is really going to benefit.

The sale of trusts and various other instruments when used correctly can be of great assistance, but they are complex and, as a result, expensive. An example of a product which serves a very useful purpose is a Lasting Power of Attorney for those who require help to bring clarity, confidence and assistance to their life, to be arranged on their behalf, and to control their finances or provide assistance with daily living as their body deteriorates or they lose mental capacity. Looking after people as they grow older and control of spending their money, as in control of life, needs to be sorted out – especially where someone relies on another person to look after their health and their wealth.

As George Best once said, "I spent money on wine, women and song… and squandered the rest". If we continue spending without checking and monitoring we cannot see where our money is being spent. Not everyone is lucky enough to be as talented as George Best, or even afford to have such a lifestyle. Without regular monitoring we are unable to establish how inflation will affect any particular element of our expenditure, or if it is likely to reduce or increase in future. We often start out with good intentions, but how many of us do not check our bank statements each month? We need to conduct regular checks and balances and keep accurate records, if only from a legal aspect.

Once decisions have been taken they cannot be easily reversed. We all make errors of judgment, whether it is working with the right people, or employing the right people, or marrying or developing a relationship with the right person.

When I started my financial planning practice, I employed people who applied for the position but the job requirements were not always right for them, or for our practice, or our clients. In the past I have not always taken on the right type of clients. In the future I may still not take on the right type of clients, but we will only know this from developing our long-term business relationship. Many of the issues stem from those who just do not engage to those who do not disclose important information (for whatever reason). This leads to a tense and annoying relationship and a breakdown of services. As a result of non-disclosure or inaccurate disclosure, we cannot meet their expectations. Clients may expect me to report back to them before obtaining accurate information or before decisions are made, and there is absolutely no point making a plan based on spurious or inaccurate information. Poor quality information in is poor quality information out. Some of our clients made use of our facilities because the cost is much lower than if they act on their own initiative based on their personal views and experiences. People pay good money for us to provide a professional service and sound advice and guidance, rather than the 'do–it–yourself' clients. A simple example is we assess each client's risk profile (especially couples), agree and set up their asset allocation accordingly, and we are looking to reduce volatility whilst retaining the opportunity to increase investment or income returns at an agreed rate.

An example is a couple where the male is the dominant character and his wife is the dominant income earner; he requires to make his own decisions on his finances, looking for opportunities to exploit and make a killing, and his wife has appointed our practice to manage her portfolio. To date the difference is minimal. The cost of constantly changing investments is reflected in his investment returns, as a result of the many additional and unnecessary ongoing charges. What he does not take into account is the research and time he spends on his computer chasing rates. Trying to second guess who or what is going to be successful is stressful and is not realistic.

One reason for this success is in-depth analysis at the outset, regular monitoring and selection of good quality asset allocation which is then transferred into good quality core funds. This process is a strategy for success, rather than following the flavour of the moment or newspaper tips and recommendations. It should be noted that newspapers are in business to sell newspapers and the sales and advertising forms a very large element of their income.

It is often said by fund managers, "If it is in the newspapers it is in the price," declaring everyone who knows about it has bought in, and as demand goes up so follows the price, making it more expensive to purchase and therefore less likely to make a profit. Many investors fail to realise there is a real time trading market with those institutions involved being ahead of the game. Other tip sheets and financial journals report on what has happened rather than focus on what you want to happen and provide a strategy to achieve it.

Insurance, unit trust and investment trust companies provide regular contributions to all sections of the press by way of reports and features where the information is sales oriented and the presentation material, even after they have conducted due diligence, is out of date. Your finances need to be fundamental, simple and back to basics, with an investigation to identify the right type of asset allocation, the correct investment product, and correct type of assets to balance your portfolio – for you.

Reader Focus Questions

Ask yourself

Proper in-depth analysis and planning at the outset can prevent most of these problems occurring. Learning from our experience you can assist with the design of your lifetime cash flow planning. We are not alone; there are many good quality advisers out there and working with one will enhance your lifestyle and ease stress. Such a plan will help you meet your desired lifestyle now and throughout retirement. With proper planning you can distribute your estate effectively, in a tax-efficient manner down through your family (but only once you no longer need it) or provide for succession planning for your family business or family assets by use of the family office facility.

A clear strategy leads to peace of mind

Education and training are essential ingredients to avoid the pitfalls of tax, contract terms, changing legislation and pension scheme rules. The Chartered Insurance Institute requires a 65% pass rate for some of their insurance industry exams. Their objective is to promote the insurance industry using highly qualified advisers for the benefit of their members, and new business figures, e.g. insurance companies, who are the sponsors for most of their events. Whilst I believe education stimulates and motivates, it is the quality of the work, the accuracy of the information and the application of this knowledge which sets the standards of the best advisers ahead of the average. The benefit in turn is passed on to the client by way of sound advice, and product selection with the correct contract terms, which in turn will lead to greater customer satisfaction, confidence in the adviser, the product provider and peace of mind for the client.

I believe in exams as a means of learning and keeping track, as well as for keeping abreast of changes and keeping up to date. However, exams and qualifications should not be seen as an end in themselves. To pass an exam should be a practical exercise. Good education should stimulate and motivate, but with these new exams the option of three answers, one of which is right, is more of a gambling exercise than the real meaning of training. Obtuse questions with equally obtuse answers are irrelevant, and frankly a waste of time and effort, as much in their design as they are a waste of time for participants, and offer little benefit to customers. Many of the new breed of exams operate a tick box mentality.

Knowledge = power

This type of education and training is designed to assist the product floggers, the tied agents or banks to provide bank, building society and insurance company employees with misguided or deceptive selling. By not providing full information on a product or service, these salespeople are thereby trained to mislead or misinform and destroy the trust on which customers rely with their sales agent or service provider. One example is Equitable Life, who claimed they did not pay commissions and had up to 20% guaranteed annuity rates built into their contracts on their retirement annuity pensions, along with other companies. These companies did not explain the actual contract terms clearly. This was a mischievous marketing policy but it was the clients who were penalised. Scottish Widows had with–profits endowment and pensions mis-selling. Many insurance companies offered these products.

These were misleading sales strategies and marketing opportunities set up through the highest levels i.e. by the Board of Directors and their respective companies, to promote reckless selling, using unachievable targets and unethical practices which were unsustainable. Many products were found to be inappropriate and unsuitable for their customers and ultimately their own company's reputation. To reduce their liabilities, these insurance companies embarked on a marketing strategy using their own salespeople and some brokers and IFAs to cull these bad sales and marketing policies and to transfer them into newer products in order to minimise their insurance companies' liabilities, with many clients losing out on the massive benefits they had signed up for under contract. This generated additional costs to customers with new commissions, increased charges but with reduced benefits from the insurance companies.

We assisted one Equitable Life client to get back over £100,000 when Equitable Life salespeople and managers transferred him out of a retirement annuity product (RAP) with a 20% guaranteed annuity rate (GAR). On top of this, the old style RAP scheme rules permitted 3.5 times the annuity rate to be taken as tax-free cash i.e. 70% of the fund. The maximum under new pension products was restricted to 25% of the fund value. New style personal pensions included other restrictions, which meant a calculation of both products and client needs identified was required as a minimum, prior to giving advice.

Cash is a low-risk investment

Another area where clients fall foul is the claims made about cash accounts where the headline rate belies the contract and contract terms, and relies on a significant portion of interest or bonus after the end of a term, e.g. a year. Some require your salary to be paid in monthly or at least a minimum of £1,000 per month.

Does the headline rate really offer true value for money?

Does the headline rate exceed inflation? If not the real value of your money will reduce in real terms i.e. purchasing power. That is the risk which needs to be identified against any benefits of access or restrictions on access.

We make judgment calls based on our own knowledge and experience and the due diligence we carry out as individuals. As an adviser, the quality of any due diligence is a means of secondary checks and balances which ensures we provide appropriate advice going forward. During this process it is important to back test to see the different outcomes of assets in different scenarios. It is important to work with your own financial planner to set out your aims and objectives, your aspirations and also make suitable flexible contingency plans. A catastrophe will make a significant impact on your dreams, so be prepared.

However, emotions do make a big impact on our decisions but it is important to remove as much emotion from the decision as possible. For this reason, write down what you want the product or service to do for you. Having a clear vision of what you want provides knowledge and peace of mind.

CHAPTER 5:
Markets are always going to be volatile

When investing, markets are always going to be volatile. Different markets work in different ways and each class of asset offers various types of risks against any potential return. The stock market is driven by fear and greed. For those investors who are hungry for the best returns there is a tendency to be greedy, without assessing what their real objective is to be, or deciding how much loss they are willing to accept. Focusing on only 'the best returns' is a recipe for disaster. I believe this type of investor to be nothing more than a gambler – and with the same consequences of losing money or chasing gains, or attempting to recover losses or searching for the next potential winner.

There is a time when returns will be required or the asset allocation or the levels or types of risk involved are secondary. The main claim of seeking out the best returns is fundamentally flawed because of the inherent risk.

Newspapers are often the source of information provided by a company or their broker, or other associated third party, or a fund manager – who provides the sales information to influence the market and its "followers", to promote their product. Journalists and reporters who provide "tips" or recommendations, and their reports, need to be more fully investigated for accuracy and validity, and any opportunity that exists.

It should be remembered that a newspaper is in business to sell newspapers and sponsored by advertising budgets of insurance companies, banks and investment fund managers – whose aim is to promote and encourage others to purchase their product.

By looking at your fundamentals and deciding on your requirements you can establish the level of risk you are willing to take. Many people buy into funds which are already doing well; buying in when the markets have moved up, and the benefits are built into the price making them expensive to purchase. This is known generally as the 'herd instinct', where investors follow the markets. As a share is found to be attractive, investors buy in pushing the price higher; once investors see profit and perceive little upside or added value, they sell which starts pushing the market price down.

One way to offset this risk is to buy into a passive or market index tracker fund. These are often sold because of reduced charges as you are not paying for fund management or for research and selection of a range of companies. Instead you rely on merely technology, buying and selling companies in the chosen index. You buy into an index and follow it up or down. With many of these tracker funds you do not have asset allocation; the fund buys into the index in the market and sells out of the market to track their desired index. As there are costs involved, they usually track just below the market index.

Couples in particular need to assess their own individual risk profile and their requirements to make the correct asset allocation which is suitable for them. Each individual has different priorities and attitude to risk – and a different willingness to offload the risk. This needs to be accounted for.

Each partner also has their own behavioural risk and this is based on the economics and each individual's view of macro and micro economics, and their personal experience.

The example of commission-hungry salespeople is an unwelcome menace as they are trained to target the unwary, vulnerable, or susceptible in their quest for their product flogging for commissions, or to reach their sponsors' targets. These menacing mercenaries in money can destroy years of prudent saving or financial planning and create havoc for the unsuspecting. Examples of these are low-cost endowments as their most serious mis-selling.

The effect of the charges on their products leads to substantial drag on market and investment returns and significant losses from upfront charges and severe penalties for early exit. For those couples who have conducted a cash flow using their income and their expenditure and looked at the way inflation will affect each area of their finances, intrusion or implementation of further products will have an impact on your plans. It is wise, therefore, to decide on your priorities with the assistance of a good financial planner, and review it each year and monitor the advice and the returns regularly.

There are reasons for volatility. Usually it is as a result of scarcity: too many people chasing too few items, e.g. shares in the market. When a company performs well their share price goes up because many investors wish to share in the company success. These investors see dividend, or dividend potential and potential for an increasing share price. If market volatility comes about as a result of greed, there are too many buyers, for whatever reason, then the price increases. If there are too few, investors or dividends drop and investors sell, so the share price reduces.

When reviewing your finances, your objectives and your priorities, you must write it down. I am a great believer in writing it down. If it is not in writing it does not happen. It is important to have something to compare against – something which is realistic for savings. It could be cash as an amount and interest rate, or it could be FTSE 100 Index and the index rate at that time. A written value allows you to check the results, to monitor your success, or otherwise.

Whatever you choose it has to demonstrate the real value of your money – the real return after charges.

> If you hold money on deposit with an interest rate of 1% (gross), you pay tax on the interest, which is taken from your interest payable by the bank or building society. You then need to report this to the HMRC and you are accountable for any higher rate of tax liability on the interest.
>
> More importantly, if inflation is higher than your interest rate – the real value of your money (known as the purchasing power) is reduced, and this effect will be compounded over time.

I recently met someone who is a 40% taxpayer who keeps £131,000 in a building society account and £90,000 in a Post Office bond. When we discussed the reason behind her decision it was due to the fact she was not sure on where to invest. Her husband used to deal with the finances and she left matters to him. Doing nothing is not an option. Many people find themselves in this situation, one partner deals in the main with all financial matters. When they are gone it leaves a hole and anxiety and fear, and many are unsure as to who to trust so they do nothing. In this case, we embarked on our Academy for Finance to develop a greater understanding of how money works – simple straightforward investing principles with constant monitoring. Now the lady has built up her confidence and thoroughly enjoys her money, how it works and how to obtain more efficient returns. No longer is she concerned about finances.

CHAPTER 6:
Define your objectives, your needs and your goals

As you learn what you want out of life, you can now decide how to best achieve this and to ensure you have sufficient money to pay for the lifestyle you wish to enjoy, now and throughout retirement.

One of the great differences in being a couple is, having been a single person with only yourself to look out for, you now have to share, to accommodate and to compromise. Each partner has their own views, their own aspirations and their own goals. For some it may be children and family home. For others it may be promotion or change of jobs. Differences in age, careers, jobs and lifestyles all combine to make you take decisions and compromise becomes much more complex. More opportunities, easier travel and job opportunities compounded with flexible transport make decisions more difficult. Lifestyles where family may have travelled abroad for better job opportunities mean couples and parents may need to build into their lifestyle financial plan the need to go abroad to visit their family to see their children and their grandchildren – and may even wish to retire to this new land to share in the new world, new family experience.

We need to look at the background in economics and the inflation rate to see how your lives will be affected by this. For example, interest rates are currently at an all-time low. Inflation whilst creeping up remains relatively low until you look more closely at wages, electricity and food and take each of these independently. By establishing your expenditure in each area you are able to see how your expenditure is affected by increased costs in raw materials or increases in electricity, which will have increased with significant differences, which affects the pound in your pocket.

Before you can look at each of these areas, you need to start with an end in mind. Define your objectives, write down your aspirations, set out your desired lifestyle. By establishing your lifestyle at the outset you can prioritise your areas which are attainable and by setting out your desires you can see if they are reasonable. Establishing objectives in a clear way and having a process to measure them means you are much more likely to attain these. If you fall short, does it matter?

Your goals and objectives do not need to be financial. Money is only a means of keeping count, a means for comparing outcomes. It could be you wish to play for your country at your best sport. You may wish to go bungee jumping from a hot air balloon for added excitement. A friend of mine tells the story of his wishing to go bungee jumping and was persuaded to do it in a hot air balloon. He had not appreciated the effect the loss of weight had when he jumped out of the balloon. As a result of weight loss, the balloon becomes lighter and the balloon went up – whilst he was going down. When the elastic tightened, his weight was then added to the balloon, which forced the balloon to go down with the added weight as he came back up. The loss of his weight to the balloon meant the balloon went back up again and this carried on like a ping pong ball – at a significant height and for some time. What he had also failed to realise was the balloon was always in the air, which meant he was stranded hanging below a hot air balloon until they stopped playing ping pong, stabilised and the balloon could be brought down to earth safely. He was not expecting that additional adrenalin rush over and above the adrenalin rush of a bungee jump. Asked if he would do it again now he knew what was involved, he said it was highly unlikely. I've done that, move on, and frankly who could blame him?

Why define your objectives – build your case?

The benefit of identifying your objectives means you are identifying what you want rather than having a wish list.

I believe everyone should have an objective – for the short term, the medium and the long term. However, this can become cumbersome and complex which can often lead to becoming tedious, or boring. If you are concerned, we often recommend a five-year plan, and it should be on one page of a piece of paper.

Goals and objectives may be job or increased career opportunities. This may be monitored by the level of salary on offer.

Goals and objectives may be your first home. You may have a wish to own a sports car; a wish becomes an objective when you write down your objective and make a plan on how you intend to achieve your objective i.e. own your sports car. You may wish to build your own business. You may wish to spend your time travelling, seeing foreign parts or more of the United Kingdom. You may wish to find a holiday home.

When purchasing a property you will need to identify where you wish to live, and why. You need to look at the costs of buying your first home: estate agents' fees, solicitors' fees, stamp duty (often omitted) and the cost of moving. You need to identify the cost of your mortgage debt over the length of the term of your mortgage debt. How much will such a slice of your monthly income be, firstly as a percentage but more importantly in monetary amount? How much are you left with in money terms? Then ask yourself can you afford to live? What would happen if you then wish to start a family, and when? How will your finances be affected? How will this affect your living standards? Are you prepared for these changes – financial, emotional, and your health by way of stress, anxiety etc.?

> For those who separate or divorce, they will have additional financial issues as a result. Where property is involved, if the first partner remains in the family home with children, and the other partner moves in with their new partner (who may also have family) there follows a massive financial exercise, long discussions – and more complex family arrangements.

How can you protect yourself against catastrophe?

Before you look at purchasing it is often a good opportunity to find your reason for purchasing i.e. the cost and advantages and benefits of renting, or living at home, and the cost and advantages and benefits of purchasing. The ongoing cost of purchasing such as repairs, improvements etc. The cost of purchasing over a 25-year mortgage debt, and any repercussions of marriage or partner break-up and the financial implications.

Once you have developed your aims and objectives, you need to put in place a strategy and a process to meet your objectives. We need to question the reasons behind our decisions to identify our need, through to the final benefit and outcome. To do this I use the words of Mr Kipling… whose words are 'exceedingly good'!

I KEEP six honest serving-men
(They taught me all I knew);
*Their names are **What** and **Why** and **When***
*And **How** and **Where** and **Who**.*
I send them over land and sea,
I send them east and west;
But after they have worked for me,
I give them all a rest.

RUDYARD KIPLING

Hobbies and holidays and travel are all good for the mind, expand our knowledge and widen our experiences and usually form an integral part of our lives. With the lower cost of travel and many more destinations, we find routes and areas expanding beyond their original state and normal boundaries to accommodate more tourists and generate more income for the area, but with it come additional problems of being overdone, overcrowded and exploitation of society, local customs and areas of scenic beauty.

However, designing your lifestyle to meet your requirements and to fulfil your enjoyment it is important to prioritise your aspirations, calculate the amount of money you will need and make provision for the quality of life you wish to achieve. This may be in your thirties, forties, fifties or into retirement.

CASE STUDY

One couple remained together for their children but now one of them has met a new partner and moved in. Children from marriage: one daughter at university and a son finishing his A levels.

The man remains in the family home, for the benefit of the children. The woman has moved out and purchased a new home for her and her new partner.

Currently, they are looking at their existing finances, to divide up their estate in a reasonable and sensible way. Unfortunately each partner is restricted in many ways. The man is self employed, and the woman has her assets tied up in the family home.

We have set up trusts for the children, into which each parent has contributed. These are to protect and secure their education and to provide for them up to age 25.

The woman is employed although job security is a concern, which may impact on their new property purchase. More importantly their property is high risk and they cannot easily get access to their capital.

We conducted a full financial planning report, with income and expenditure for both independently to identify their lifetime cashflow, and carried out several "what if" scenarios using the Prestwood Financial Planning system.

We have found the man (self employed) needs to get out and find business, and we are assisting him in his efforts through sales and marketing, local advertising etc., and developed his business plan.

The woman and her new partner are starting life in a precarious position financially. Effectively starting again so life assurance and permanent health protection are important (for both), to provide finances in the event of sickness and/or accident. We are using a PHI contract and a sickness and accident protection product along with a term assurance contract to protect their asset and their income. That is what insurance is designed for and what it does.

Interestingly the building society did "not require" life assurance or sickness and accident policies to be set up. A cynical person might believe this is due to the fact that if one partner died or became ill, the lender would reclaim their property and sell it on – as they have no interest in the family or their finances – only the return of their investment.

After conducting our professional fact find and analysis – we set up the Family Trust for the children to protect their interests. This in case any new partnerships did not work out and claims were made against the original partners.

Life Assurance and sickness and accident protection for the woman and her partner, and the sale of the family home in 18 month's, allows time for the man to get financially well organised and he may decide to pay a rental income to his ex-wife for her share, under a legally binding contract.

To do this we checked their income and assessed their tax liability before designing a suitable financial plan for each partner. Once agreed we monitor the plan, check and validate and constantly update it once a year under our annual review requirement. Their new Wills formed the basis of each plan, and the peace of mind brought to each partner (and the new man) showed me just how good and how rewarding working with people in close liaison, engagement, discussion, and compromise can be for all.

What was a laissez-faire family relationship had become more independent and more focussed and each partner was now more involved, to find their own solution, to find a new beginning and develop their own new desired lifestyle.

Put simply, we utilise many professional strategies and in this case we are including and following our Lifesmart® Financial Plan, which incorporates, "the 7 ages of financial health" by Dr Jack Oliver (FT and Pitman publishing) which demonstrates the various financial requirements at each age.

Together they discovered, how to identify and write down their views, write down their aims and objectives and write down their desired lifestyles, as our starting point. Together we developed a plan with sound financing through a solid income and expenditure as their current cashflow, and our Lifesmart® Lifetime cashflow, development. If they overspent on one area it showed the impact it will have on other areas of their finances and the impact on their desired lifestyle.

It is important to identify first and foremost your time management.

Once you have integrated time management into your schedule, life becomes more organised, more efficient and more effective.

Now you need to decide your worth. What value do you place upon your time? Will others be willing to pay that amount? If not, does that matter? Financial planning as an example is all about interaction, engagement and implementation.

There is absolutely no point going through the fundamentals if you prevaricate, defer and do not implement your plan. Put simply, you are wasting your own time as well as everyone else's. In our service you will have paid us already, so there is no further financial consideration to take into account.

Putting a value on your time focuses the mind. It does not really matter if the value seems inappropriate or even extortionate. The function behind such an amount is it is only your means of keeping count. It is really important to assess your worth in financial or monetary terms.

I recall the reaction of one of my managers at Scottish Widows when I was explaining to him that my time spent with him was of less value to the company and to me as I was being deprived of being in front of my customers – the IFAs, tied agents, brokers, accountants and solicitors who held agencies with Scottish Widows. I had some 800 agencies in my area.

I was given unachievable targets, and no opportunity to make any bonus on top of my salary, although was at the top end of the salary range, so the company pension contribution remained unaffected. I also contributed personally with tax relief. I explained to my manager my time was worth £100 per hour as my means of keeping count. I had learned this idea from one of the industry greats. My manager first accused me of charging 'his agents' for my time, and was not amused when I jokingly suggested that if this was truly the case I should send him an invoice! The amusement was not transferable. The manager could not understand why time lost could not be made up, and caused additional and unnecessary time constraints, anxiety and stress to complete our tasks.

To this day I still do not think the manager 'got it'. The point is when you check and monitor your effectiveness you need something to monitor it with. You need something to monitor against – and money is a good means of keeping count. I currently use £250 per hour and I deal with barristers who have hourly rates in excess of £5,000 per hour. Why? Because they are worth it. The real value for money is not in the amount you charge but in the outcomes achieved and the total return for clients. The total return is not just for finance, but could be for achieving their goal of a good holiday once a year, or some other easily identified aim or objective.

Using a financial hourly rate allows you to identify when you are spending your time inefficiently and ineffectively.

CHAPTER 7:
Taking responsibility for your finances

By deciding on your objectives and your desires and the process and procedures you will adopt, it is important to put in place your strategy to meet them.

Whether we like it or not, we each need to take full responsibility for our finances. We take responsibility on how and where we spend our money but banks and financial institutions are arrogant, reckless with our funds and most of all time-consuming.

If you work on the basis the bank has your money and is determined to tell you how best to use your money for their best interests you will not be far out!

Banks and insurance companies are in general very friendly yet most unhelpful in the area of their advice, which clients require but which is restricted. Banks and financial institutions need your money for their purposes. The banks and building societies and other financial institutions are intent on taking over control of your money and telling you what you can or cannot do with it whilst charging for their poor quality, generally abysmal banking services and poor customer service. Banks are now outsourcing their administration to India and other call centres, leaving a poor level of expertise of bank employees who have little or no access to a reasonable banking programme to provide a basic service.

I was speaking to a lady of 87 who went into the bank to get £200 out. The insensitive bank employee recommended she go outside to their hole-in-the-wall machine and do the transaction herself as she would not need to wait in the queue.

A senior police officer instructed the bank he needed £12,000 out in cash to pay for a deposit on a car. The bank was given four days' notice, and he confirmed with the bank official that he would come in with his wife at 11am on the day. They arrived on time to be told the bank had not obtained any permission, and put simply, as a result of their slovenly service they were not ready. The bank, Santander, confirmed they had the money in the bank but it was some 45 minutes of waiting before it was brought out in sealed envelopes. The police officer requested they go into a quiet room for privacy out of reach of prying eyes, to count out the amount and ensure it was accurate. The bank employee refused and counted it out at the counter in full sight of anyone entering the bank. It took over 55 minutes after the original appointment for Santander's 'banking service' to provide the cash and the bank had made their customer a potential target after they left the premises – a result of an untrained, incompetent bank employee, and lack of any managerial controls. These are the unintended consequences of the actions by untrained and thoughtless bank employees.

I personally took £200 cash out of the machine at the Bank of Scotland in Perth. This Lloyds TSB owned Halifax Bank of Scotland refused to exchange the highly decorative Scottish notes for English notes, which I requested as I was returning to England later that day. The bank employees from the teller to the bank manager confirmed I needed a Bank of Scotland account to pay the money into before being able to take the money out again in English currency, rather than execute a simple exchange of these Scottish notes for English notes. I asked for verification of this in writing and I received written confirmation on the processes and procedures of this tardy bank. I had both my passport and the receipt from the Bank of Scotland cash machine. Such incredible stupidity for such a simple banking transaction. It is my theory that the Bank of Scotland wanted to charge me for exchanging their Scottish money for English money, as they are commercial money lenders.

In my opinion, the HBOS teller made a poor judgment call on the basis I was not a HBOS client, and had no evidence other than the HBOS bank note confirming my bank account and branch. I believe HBOS directives are to prevent interbank arrangements, as a result of their restrictive practices, to inconvenience and create unnecessary hassle for consumers, resulting in poor quality of banking services and in a breach of the Banking Code of Practice and FCA rules.

When I tried to withdraw my own money from my Bank of Scotland business account, I was transferred to a Glasgow call centre, as a consequence of having no branches in my area. The closest branch of the Halifax Bank of Scotland is over 30 miles away in London. I had to telephone the Glasgow Call centre and one of their 40 bank managers sent a message to their owners, Halifax, at the Halifax branch in St Albans, Hertfordshire. I then had to attend the branch in person with my passport, cheque book and reference number and waited over 35 minutes – which is how long it took each time for the Halifax's poor quality branch managers and employees to provide my money in cash. These inefficient and frustrating delays have not been explained to this day.

This is not what I could refer to as "convenience", or "convenient" banking from the owners LloydsTSB who owned Halifax Bank of Scotland (HBoS) at the time.

In these financial services companies it is not what you know, it is what you do not know which makes the difference.

Taking any advice from any bank or financial institution should be simple. However, they have made contracts ever more complex to drive lethargy and derive acceptance from clients. The strategy is to bully customers into accepting the bank and insurance companies' poor levels of service, poor propositions, and poor quality of employees who are often untrained, unhelpful and are providing a poor client experience. One reason for this poor quality is the banks and building societies are playing a numbers game, in my opinion exploiting their clients, and their sums do not add up.

These tactics are restrictive trade practices, which the Bank of England has not dealt with. It suggests these banks are not fit for purpose, for which only the Bank of England and their Regulation, after full investigation, can decide.

Taking advice

Taking advice is about gaining access to, and paying directly for, competent, professional, qualified, skilled, experienced and most importantly an independent and trusted adviser.

For the advice to be valuable, you must first accept it and secondly be responsible for it. To be successful you need to take action and implement the advice.

It is of the highest importance that you agree the terms of business upfront and the level of service you require, and your trusted adviser's remuneration should be discussed and agreed in advance after it has been explained, and prior to any advice on offer.

It is of the highest priority that you confirm what you wish to achieve with your trusted adviser and to work together to define your objectives from the outset. This process will ensure better client outcomes.

It is of the highest priority that you provide your adviser with all the relevant information required and agree the assumptions used in your calculations, to properly determine and formulate your written financial plan. These assumptions allow the adviser to analyse and recommend the most effective and efficient way forward, now and for the future. Such a calculation will be the basis of your lifetime cash flow to ensure you do not run out of money. It would be perverse if an adviser, having been given all the relevant and accurate information, agreed the assumptions but was ignored by the client who followed their own path – especially after having agreed to pay.

In the past I have had experiences where we are not given the full disclosure of information upfront. As a result, we now operate a facility where we ask all the relevant questions and, where necessary, we need to delve further and deeper to ask questions to identify and obtain full disclosure. This is needed to assess the quality and accuracy of the information provided to ensure it adds up. It is worth remembering an adviser's reputation is on the line if it is found to be inaccurate or false information provided. It is important to assess the actual desire or real attitude into their statements or into taking a risk and of how much risk a client would be comfortable with. The objective for the adviser is client peace of mind. A good adviser will require you to supply full information on your requirements. In return your adviser will advise, based on the information you provide, which should in turn provide a suitable recommendation upon which you should have trust and confidence. It is this trust which is so essential in any relationship, whether personal or in business.

It is the great trust developed between adviser and client which is not easy to replicate from banks and other financial institutions due mainly to the fact that they remain product floggers for the masses rather than being committed to the customer's best outcomes or providing a proper service. It is by manipulating contracts sold through their advisers – in many instances without their knowledge – which has exploited the untrained, inexperienced adviser to sell 'bad' products to the gullible and unsuspecting public. It is similar to Tesco selling horsemeat in their advertised 'beef' burgers. It may not have harmed anyone to any great degree but the product provider misled people through their advertising and lack of monitoring or controls. Unfortunately, in the case of endowments, the repercussions had more serious financial implications for their clients, and the endowment policy has earned a bad reputation for both the product and the insurance companies involved as a consequence.

Ironically, the endowment policy had, and still has, many good characteristics but why would any reasonable salesperson go out of their way, or take on the added time costs and client discussions through to arguments to sell such a product? Nowadays, with new advances in technology, many other opportunities have arisen and their product-flogging salesperson may no longer be required. Over the decades we have experienced the breakdown of the most vital element of the business relationship: TRUST by banks and insurance companies as a result of the great mis-selling (misleading) scandals in endowments, pensions and other financial products such as PPI sold by product providers. This, together with the fortunes lost by clients in charges, expenses and commissions, has destroyed confidence in these tardy, unprofessional and unethical financial institutions. With this in mind you may need to find yourself a new model of adviser. I recommend you find a trusted adviser who acts in your best interests, who you pay directly, and who is not tied to any one (or more) companies or restricted in the services they sell. Those tied and restricted agents may try and claim an element of independence or claim to be 'nearly independent' on the product-flogging side of their business but remain remunerated by commissions or payments by their sponsoring company. This can apply whether under a self-employed contract, or a contract of service as an employee acting for and on behalf of his/ her employer, or acting as an agent for the bank or insurance company.

To offer independent and impartial advice, I believe your trusted adviser has to be able to demonstrate impartiality – free from bias or of any influence such as commissions, free holidays, free office space, use of company sponsored implements such as telephones, photocopiers, computers and computer systems, etc. Openness and transparency are crucial in the conduct of the trusted adviser's business, and are essential along with the 'fee for advice' received as an integral part of their contract with you. I believe this to be the way of an ethical trusted adviser with open, transparent and ethical business practices.

Some high street Independent Financial Advisers (IFAs) may claim to be 'independent', although it is important to establish how independent they really are. Do they only deal with a small amount of business and are therefore restricted to one or two product providers (often insurance companies) who remunerate them by way of commissions, which are deducted from your investment product? Some may pay higher than normal commissions depending on volume of business, or other targets. Alternatively they may receive lunches, dinners or some other interactive or engaging activity, or invitations to sporting events. The question to ask is do they receive benefits or other inducements, e.g. offers to attend golf days which may help and influence their decisions on your business?

I like to be impartial, be seen to be impartial, and remain impartial. I operate my business with companies who can provide an additional level of technical knowledge above and beyond the basic knowledge of the semi-skilled employees who are given targets and rewarded by their sponsor as a result of their sales pitch. I only work with companies who operate on an ethical and professional basis in a clear, transparent and open manner. Quite apart from anything else, it saves so much valuable time for everyone.

To look at your finances and take responsibility for them, you have taken this step by setting out your objectives and laying out your goals in writing. Without an objective and without a goal means you have no control or reason to respond or reply. Put simply, you have no substance to your objective. It is, therefore, only a wish.

If you set unrealistic or unattainable objectives and fail to reach them it may not be very motivating, but it may be no bad thing. It could just be that you have been overambitious. You may just have set your goals too high, but if you have fallen short it may be all right because you will at least have achieved more than you would have done by not setting any goals at all and having no set objectives.

Life's journey

Life is often referred to as 'a journey' by many product providers in the advertising pitches of their sales and marketing departments which are designed to sell you a product. If you look behind the analogy and at the process prior to a journey, by whichever method, to your destination, it follows a simple process.

You select where you want to go, and why. You establish the reason for the visit: business or pleasure. Then you look at various options: road, rail, sea or air travel. Then you look at the cost and value for money of each type of transport. Once these have been decided you look at the additional costs, e.g. parking and ease with which you can get to the airport. Time restrictions: do you have to be at the airport two hours before the flight? What will you do with those two hours in the airport?

If you have decided to fly to save time, you turn up at the airport, go through security, wait in various queues, and board the plane when instructed. The pilot has been on the aircraft for some time, and carried out his routine checks, safety checks, instrument checks and aircraft checks. The amount of fuel is sufficient, the flight path mapped, and repeated checks with the tower are made to ensure all is well. Weather conditions are checked to see if they have any impact and any changes need making. All this work is carried out prior to the journey, without your knowledge, and you take off and arrive at your destination.

Embarking on a journey, most people make their own travel arrangements. You can ask someone else to make the arrangements for you, e.g. a business owner might ask his/her personal assistant or individuals may ask a travel agent and pay them for their work accordingly. However, travel is very personal and it is likely you will wish to be fully involved. You will challenge your decisions, e.g. on type of travel: road, rail, sea or air. For the journey you will drill down into your requirements, food, seats, things to do, length of time it will take etc., you will discuss with others, perhaps, and ask for a second opinion, for reassurance, all for the sake of a journey.

Given the above, why do we not take the same responsibility for our finances?

I believe that apathy and fear play the biggest part in people's failure to take responsibility for their actions, whether in finance or sometimes in other areas of their life. Many people fail to take control because of their apathy and their fear of the unknown, and finances are often overly complicated and do not appear to be fun. A lack of confidence and a lack of trust in advisers has seen the resurrection of others, and the reintroduction of the 'pub adviser'. A recent report showed that people were willing to take advice from their friends, or from newspaper and magazine articles which were often out of date, inaccurate or plain wrong. Furthermore they did not take into account the various aspects such as economics, inflation or attitude to risk. The lack of knowledge, the complications, and the hassle also proved to be a deterrent.

This is an industry which thrives and survives by people's laziness and apathy to promote their expensive products. One great misnomer is Premium Bonds which offer the purchaser the chance to win a variety of monthly tax-free jackpots, where the opportunity to win, along with the return of original capital, overshadows the other side of such an investment, the return and the rest of the product. National Savings and Investments (NS&I) is one of the oldest savings institutions in the UK. All NS&I products carry a government guarantee, which means they rank as one of the most secure investments available. They could have a significant part to play in your overall financial portfolio.

Designing your own lifestyle

Lifestyle is most important to everyone. You need to have fun. It is important to make your objectives clear and provide ways and means of achieving these in the most convenient and pleasant manner.

Objectives do not just have to be reasonable, attainable and measureable, they must also be pleasurable. Your objectives have to be fun and show it's a pleasure dealing with you or doing business with you.

There are financial planners, or financial coaches, who are specialist people on hand to assist you, who can help you decide and direct you and help you focus on what is important. Financial planners assist to put you back on track when you stray. These specialists help you to discuss and assess the importance of each action and the direction which offers most opportunity, to help you on your journey and your destination. After setting your objectives it is important to be focused on your finances. By dealing with your finances more fully each year there is less need to chop and change products or investments. Many financial institutions and advisers make huge profits by swapping and changing your funds at your cost. There may be good reasons behind these changes but there can also be an element of churning, usually for commissions. Churning is the term used by the Financial Conduct Authority (FCA) for switching funds or products without good reason or explanation, or identifying the actual costs i.e. charges and risk with such a strategy. One reason for churning is to gain additional commissions by an authorised adviser from the product provider.

Having set your goals and objectives you need to address your attitude to risk. When assessing risk for couples you need to look at each individual's willingness to take risk. Risk needs to be addressed in the short term, the medium term and over the longer term. Risk can be reduced by the length of time you wish to invest. Once you have decided on the level of risk you are willing to take, it is important to decide on how much you can afford to lose. We describe this as your capacity for loss. When you are young your capacity for loss can be greater as you have a lifetime within which to plan and monitor. As you progress through to later life you may not wish to take risk because you have little opportunity to redress an error.

Advisers

With so many advisers and people offering to 'look after your money', I have found many advisers do not listen to you, preferring instead to set out their own views of what you should want to achieve – usually to direct you and to promote and sell their product or service.

Some advisers use large amounts of jargon to entertain their own egos and make the sale more complex than it actually is. This is often a means to demonstrate how awfully clever they are, and how awfully stupid their client is. Fortunately, most people have a grip on reality, have oodles of common sense and just need assistance with the direction or demystifying the jargon. You are not alone, you are not stupid and a good adviser will stay in touch with reality and assist you to take the route which is best and most appropriate and which serves you – whether in finance or health or fitness. As a result of being paid commissions directly from their sponsors, some advisers may take the route of least resistance. By this I mean their objective is to sell a product in order to receive their commission. This may mean a poor fact find or a desire to sell any product to allow them to move on to their next client. As a result this may not be the most suitable product or the provision of sound advice which may involve more lengthy discussions.

Sometimes it really is just a case of providing some reassurance that the clients are not making a mistake or they require a fuller explanation of the product; the advantages and the disadvantages may need to be discussed. It is always most worthwhile to balance the benefits of a product or service against the cost as these are for the long term and essential ingredients in protecting your personal wealth.

Offloading risk

When assessing risk the first area to address is why do you need to take risk? Can you offload the risk on to others? We all do this already by purchasing car insurance and house insurance. Car insurance is compulsory and is a legal requirement but many people fail to see the major benefits of protecting your car as an asset and protecting against the potential liability you could be exposed to in an accident or running someone over. All this protection through the purchase of car insurance; for example, if you have an accident and someone is knocked over and they are injured or become impaired for life, with car insurance it is the insurer who will pay for the cost rather than the individual being sued, to the full extent of their assets.

We decide whether we want full comprehensive cover, or third party, fire and theft, or third party only. We decide and compromise and balance the cost of comprehensive against third party insurance claims. People forget (or do not learn) they are protecting themselves, their assets, the car or house, or their contents, and if someone is injured the liability of the insurance company means they are contracted to pay out on specific reasonable events, e.g. someone being run over by the driver of a car, an accident or mechanical malfunction and the car goes up in flames. Home insurance is also used in the same way and you can add accidental insurance to cover accidents in the home or the normal insurance of a bedroom-rated policy which is more general and usually offered by mortgage lenders. Insurance is not designed to provide a profit after a catastrophic event but to share the risk with others, to put you back into roughly the same position.

You can look at offloading the risk on various liabilities such as public and product liability. For businesses, employer and employee liability covers for the cost of a claim and the victim of an accident. Clearly the insurance company will assess if there has been negligence on the part of the insured – whether employer, or the driver of a car, or owner of a house – and assess if the owner of their insurance policy should make a claim, and how much responsibility they should have for the accident or event.

Risk is taken on by insurance companies on the likelihood of a specific event. Once the risk is taken on by insurance companies, they spread the risk on to other third parties. This helps them to limit their liability, and help them in pursuit of their profit. These insurance companies go to great lengths to assess the risks involved and the type of individual – whether competent, committed or reckless. Have there been previous claims, what are the reasons behind each claim? In most instances insurance companies will make every attempt to pay out on all reasonable claims. Unfortunately, some people see the insurance as a means of gaining an unfair financial advantage rather than protecting their asset against loss. These claims can be simply innocent ignorance, or a variety of deceit through to attempted fraud. Those who do not think the insurance company will care are sadly wrong. Insurance companies have management and shareholders to answer to, as well as regulators and the law.

The main benefit of passing the risk on to a third party is the peace of mind in the event of an accident, rather than take the risk on your own, in full and without compromise. It is after all your own personal wealth which is at risk. By using an insurance or assurance policy you are spreading the risk. Taking out a policy does not remove your responsibility to look after your assets.

Life assurance

Life assurance offers protection on the life of an individual or a couple. By purchasing a life assurance policy the person is insured along with many others to provide protection for the life assured. The life assurance is called the sums assured. The sums assured are the right amount of money required, as agreed by client and adviser during their assessment, in the event of a catastrophe such as untimely death, sickness or accident, or critical illness.

Put simply, an amount of money, the sum assured, is paid out as a lump sum on death or critical illness, or a monthly amount in the event of long-term or permanent illness.

If the life assured meets with an untimely death it can have the most serious financial consequences on their partner and their family. A life assurance policy should pay out on premature or untimely death. A life assurance policy should provide the right amount of money in the right hands at the right time, in return for a regular premium assessed prior to taking out a policy and after consideration of many variables, such as age and health.

Mortgage and the family business

One of the most important considerations is to take on mortgage debt. The purchase of your residential property is a major consideration, along with the cost of purchase such as solicitors' and estate agents' fees, stamp duty and the time spent looking for the right property.

One of the largest purchases in our lives will be the purchase of a property and the implications it has on families and family finances. When property is purchased it becomes an asset and often it commences with the purchase of a small flat, followed by a larger flat with more bedrooms, or a small house, then a larger family house as your career and family develops, before downsizing as you get older and offspring have moved away and started their own families.

Many people use the family home as part of their retirement planning together with any other investments and assets to produce an income in addition to the State Pension Scheme.

One area which causes financial strain is where a family member dies and the child or children may need to be looked after by guardians, usually another family member, a sister or brother or sometimes their parents. With marriage break-up on the increase, family issues like this are much more common. It is essential to give consideration to a catastrophe such as death and the financial impact on the family and family finances and use 'what if' scenarios and testing for such events. Put simply, the effect both financially and emotionally.

If parents die together who will be the guardian(s) of the children?

- Have you asked the potential guardian?

- Will they accept the responsibility?

- What are the financial consequences for the guardian(s)?

If you have a mortgage and one partner dies, what will happen to the mortgage debt? It is worth   remembering all debts need to be repaid before probate is granted.

Will

It is essential to have made a valid Will. In your Will you will give direction: your instructions with regard to what has to happen to your children, who you wish to appoint as guardians and how your estate is to be distributed. It is essential to make financial provision for children, especially those under age 18, and a simple life assurance can be set up with an appropriate trust, with the executors and trustees appointed to look after funds for the benefit of the child, up to age 25.

The peace of mind brought about by being financially well organised and by adopting this strategy means less financial strain on the guardians. Such an action and putting in place a financial strategy now and for the future means your children are catered for in the event of a catastrophe such as premature death, accident or illness. Alternatively you may wish to make provision in your absence for education, university or contemplation of marriage. Writing a valid Will brings these to the fore and allows you to make arrangements and with it organisation and peace of mind.

CASE STUDY

An example of this was two sisters who had three children and one child respectively. The relationship of the sister with one child broke down and when I was taking instructions for drafting her Will she confirmed her sister would look after her child. Her sister agreed until I asked the question, "How are you going to make financial provision for another child, for food, clothes and education?" The cost of these had not been considered. We agreed who should be the guardians; we set up a term assurance policy until the child was 18; and we set up a trust and placed the policy in the trust so the trustees could pay out income or capital as required.

The trustees have a duty to ensure they act impartially with the best interests of the child uppermost.

This is a good example of talking through the real implications and making everyone involved aware of their duties and responsibilities, and the peace of mind from having taken and implemented the necessary action.

Property

Property purchase is another emotional event. Most people have a distorted view on the value of property and assume it will continue to increase in value. However, the background to increased property prices was driven mainly by demand: the baby boomers buying a flat, then a house, then a larger three-bedroomed house, with the intention of selling it to provide additional money to fund their retirement by downsizing and retaining some cash to fund their lifestyle.

Should people purchase property and if so how? I believe you should purchase a property on the basis it is a family home. Most people cannot buy a property outright and require a commercial money lender such as a bank or building society. Basically there are two ways to purchase a property and you need a significant deposit – usually around 25%. Some lenders will allow a lower deposit but this often means more restrictions, less flexibility and higher rates of interest. You can purchase a property with a capital and interest repayment mortgage. This means you repay mainly interest in the early years and once the lender has been paid their interest you start reducing the capital outstanding. During a 25-year mortgage you usually pay off a large proportion of interest in the first five to six years, and very little capital; as with every loan, the commercial lender wants their interest paid off first. After year 12 you are mainly reducing the capital outstanding as you have paid off most of the interest. Unfortunately, we have seen parents and grandparents having paid off their mortgages taking on a mortgage to provide deposits for their children.

Taking on mortgage debt at or near retirement in my opinion is not necessarily a good idea.

The other way to repay the mortgage debt is interest only, where the borrower only pays off interest during the term of the contract and pays off the outstanding debt at the end of the term. If you fail to repay the debt before the end of the term you will pay the lender more in interest. Many endowments were sold on the back of interest-only mortgages and similar strategies were employed with pensions contracts. There is an insurance company generated sales pitch to be aware of with pension mortgages. Tax relief at basic rate is added to your pension contribution and further deduction up to higher rate tax is deducted to your highest rate. When you take benefits from your pension you can take a lower income and a tax-free lump sum at commencement of up to 25% of your pension fund under the current legislation. Some clever sales people claim you are 'getting the taxman to contribute to your mortgage repayment'. This is partially true. However, if legislation changes or you no longer have earned income you may want to stop contributions. Furthermore, if legislation changes and you are no longer able to obtain a tax-free lump sum at commencement, your financial planning will be fundamentally flawed. Furthermore, you will need to find another asset or sell your home to pay off the debt.

With interest-only mortgages one advantage is you are repaying your debt with devalued money, often in 25 years' time or whatever term of mortgage you have chosen. This means inflation may have eroded the purchasing power of the outstanding debt, the pound in your pocket. You can use various other assets or products to accumulate sufficient capital to repay the outstanding debt. Alternatively you could sell the property – but what then?

Types of mortgage

1. Capital and interest

2. Interest only

There are various product variations and types of mortgage from fixed rates, variable rates and discounted rates to choose from and it is essential to get sound professional advice from a registered, qualified and authorised mortgage adviser – your trusted mortgage adviser.

Inflation based on the Retail Price Index (RPI) and the Consumer Price Index (CPI) will impact on your finances and it is essential to build these into your financial plan. RPI is the main inflation rate and includes many items in everyday use. CPI was introduced with fewer items and, as you would expect, is lower as a result and used in insurance company projections for pensions and annuities etc.

One client we helped was someone with an old-style pension where the insurance company wanted to switch him out into their newer super-duper plan. Lower charges and more fund choice were quoted as the reason. The insurance company employee tried to convince the client he could take 25% of the fund tax free and failed to disclose he could take 33% of the fund tax free under the old policy. They also failed to disclose that the old plan had an 11% guaranteed annuity rate (GAR). The value of the old contract after the higher charges was just over £1,000,000.

We recommended he take no cash but only take income of £110,000 per annum to underpin his pension income. The disadvantage was it was on a single life basis which meant his wife would receive nothing if he died prematurely. We arranged for a £1,000,000 life assurance policy on his life (no commissions taken which reduced the cost) and paid for out of the increased annuity (pension) income. He only has to live ten years, and will probably live 30 years, with £110,000 per annum, on top of a payment of income by way of a lump sum for his wife. As a result of financial planning they had the opportunity of underpinning and guaranteeing his income, and as a result we were also able to plan for Inheritance Tax and estate planning down through their family.

CHAPTER 8:
Having fun
with finance

There is no point in protecting your assets, building up your savings and investments, unless you can enjoy your money. Having fun with your finance helps you to enjoy the lifestyle you desire, to design your life around your requirements, and work towards this. Money can help you enjoy life, and you can use your money as a means of keeping count.

By establishing your desired lifestyle, the amount of time you want to work, and the level of income you need to fund it, you can decide how and where and what you need to do to provide you with   the means to achieve that lifestyle.

You may have to compromise. You might change your work patterns or work part-time or job share or apply for more fulfilling or full-time work or aim higher up the employment ladder. It may be that when you calculate your lifetime cash flow you can afford to reduce your work levels or patterns.

CASE STUDY

I advised a professional solicitor who had been working for many years and was getting fed up with the remedial and boring type of work as well as the volume of unfulfilling work he had to deal with. Further discussions drew out that he wanted to retire – but he wanted to retire to Wales and write a book. He felt he had to keep working; it was unlikely he could sell the practice and he had three employees to consider. Once we had established his costs and expenses we carried out a cash flow model which he eventually agreed with. We looked at and analysed his income and his savings and we looked into the dispersion over the short, medium and long term. He had already made some provision for his longer term retirement pensions. These had been sold to him over the years without establishing the reason behind them, or their objective. He was surprised to discover he was still contributing into an old-style retirement annuity plan. This was where he paid the gross amount and reclaimed tax at the end of his year.

When considering financial planning you should look to protection first: protection of assets, protection of income, and protection of the family. Once this has been completed it is important to look at the long term, and address retirement planning.

This retirement annuity plan had been set up in 1979 and had increased in line with his wages at the time. He was young and keen in those days and had determination, enjoyed his work and life and had made regular savings for no particular reason, he said. A direct salesman had sold him an insurance company pension plan which commenced at £40 per month and had index linked the premiums at 15% per annum – and that had continued. What the salesperson did not disclose was the indexation was also subject to new, upfront initial charges of some 50% of first year's premium, in this case the indexation amount, paid to the adviser on an ongoing basis, plus annual ongoing commissions.

All these charges and commissions were taken from the client's pension contributions. A nice little earner for the adviser! The indexation it was claimed would keep up with inflation, but avoided a regular visit from the salesperson, which popped up every four years it seems. The salesperson has left the industry, and the insurance company continues to receive the original amount plus all the increments. This would be considered very profitable for the insurance company and a drag on the investment returns for the client. It is distressing from any adviser's point of view, and more importantly the client's, that insurance companies are so lax and uncaring – and it really is up to the client to find a good quality adviser and insurance company.

When we looked into the pension funds we were amazed at the growth in some of them. One had been in a European fund which had made tremendous returns. Another had performed well as it had benefited from regular savings. When we analysed the funds over the periods and it became clear that no checks or monitoring had taken place, and no profits taken. Losses had not been checked or sold. Put simply, there was no adviser service. More importantly, this was typical customer apathy at work.

Banks and insurance companies make a lot of money from clients and advisers investing in their default funds and leaving them without checks and without monitoring, to the financial detriment of the client. Our client had also purchased seven other policies with varying premiums. He had not checked them, just kept paying them – and worst of all no one had reviewed them since commencement. The insurance company had sent out statements, but had missed some years. The most crucial point was the client had no idea for the reason behind the products purchased, or more importantly the policies' potential outcome at his selected retirement date. When you look after the pennies, the pounds look after themselves. If our client ignores or refuses to look after his pounds, would it be any surprise if at his selected retirement date he discovered a massive shortfall? If this happens it is too late to do much about it.

To provide for a reasonable lifestyle he needed £28,000 per annum in Wales and wanted additional funds in cash in case of an emergency.

When we gathered all the information we discovered he had not reclaimed tax relief on the premiums on the retirement annuity plan. His accountant appeared to be unaware of the product. It seems as though his accountant had not asked for the information, or checked it against his bank statement. We have other clients whose accountants make a point of asking for new contracts or pension contributions as a matter of course – but if it is not forthcoming it has the same effect. This is the client's responsibility. It is important to engage with your adviser, your solicitor and your accountant in full. After our calculations, a lifetime cash flow model demonstrated that we could give him £28,000 per annum and he could retire to Wales. It was only after an in-depth research on contracts that we discovered how much was in his retirement pot, and how we could make it last until age 91. If he passed away first, his wife could continue to receive the income. Had he been in poor health we could have obtained a higher and guaranteed pension annuity.

The benefit of reviewing your desires and your aspirations and looking at your needs on an annual basis means you maintain control over your funds, your direction, and check the risk attached to each product and fund. By doing this you will meet your objectives, and if not you can decide whether you should adjust or change any aspect of your finances. Finances are a moveable feast and banks and insurance companies exploit client lethargy and their continuous tweaking of interest rates and policy contract terms – to their financial advantage and to the financial disadvantage of their clients.

I would recommend looking at the services you require, such as a current account, a deposit account and a term deposit account in the bank of your choice. This money should be classed as your cash, and be used for everyday expenses. The deposit account can be used to build up your non normal expenditure such as the cost of your family holiday fund, or short-term holidays such as a party away at a spa or some other retreat. Perhaps a few days away playing golf or fishing or a weekend break. Set aside an amount of money you feel worthwhile – for fun! A special weekend away or more. That special holiday!

Next comes your long-term requirements, which means setting aside some investments for assisting with funding in your retirement. With longer term investing, due to the time frame you can afford to be more adventurous with your choice of investment. A jolly good discussion with your adviser on your level of risk and the risk required to meet the investment returns required is a must.

Short- to medium-term investing also requires goal setting which means you need to demonstrate accurately how much money you calculate you may need, and when and for what reason. The reason can change. Such an investment requires more consideration, but New Individual Savings Accounts (NISAs) and other term investments can assist in defining how much is needed and when. Investments in this area can be tailored to suit your objective and the use of NISAs, which do not have any Capital Gains Tax, may be used to great effect by selecting the most appropriate asset class. NISAs can allow a greater level of risk for the opportunity of higher returns and require more in-depth research, inspection and monitoring. New Individual Savings (NISA) are restricted to £15,240 per annum for each individual.

It never fails to amaze me when people talk about the 'interest rate' on deposit accounts and how they have achieved a perceived 'increase' by switching accounts to pay a monthly fee for the benefit of complicated claims of 'money back' on electricity payments or some other wheeze. If you switch from an interest rate of 1% to 3% on a deposit of £10,000 (1% of £10,000 and 3 % =£100 and £300 respectively) less tax @20% = £80 and £240 respectively, or 40% (higher rate tax) which is £60 and £180 respectively. You need to decide if this is worth the hassle! If it is less than £10,000 it is even further reduced and less value for money. Scrimping to save such a miserly amount does not take into account the time spent trying to set up a new bank deposit account, which takes weeks of planning to get into a bank, hours spent with a bank employee, and the ongoing problems and issues of poor quality administration and bankers' incompetence.

Basic advice is to choose your bank wisely. Do not be influenced by the complex range of accounts or their claims, which are a distraction and the result of a serious marketing cost to the bank to attract your money, even if it is only for their short term. Banks specialise in retail marketing with many claims and associated 'benefits'. Choose your bank for quality of service rather than the array of products and bundled services they are flogging on any particular day. If the bank employee becomes obstinate then walk away. I believe that if bank directors concentrated their efforts on customer care they would become more efficient and much more effective. They would also save shareholders vast amounts of money. A good instant access account should be opened as a minimum with immediate access. This type of account provides the facility to allow you to place your income, keep an amount for an emergency, and be ready to move to the next area of your financial planning.

Money can be transferred into a higher interest account with restrictions which may offer a higher rate of interest. For those with more than the current personal allowance of £10,600, income tax on savings is likely to have a greater impact. By selecting the most appropriate product by its tax status this should provide for more effective and efficient investing. You will be taxed according to your tax code at your respective rate. Each partner has a personal allowance and these may be used to your advantage.

Cash held in Individual Savings Accounts (ISAs) can offer tax-free savings up to £5,348 and these can be used to provide tax-free interest and tax-free growth or tax-free income. These along with the equity-based ISAs provide many efficient opportunities for planning and reducing tax and providing for an income in retirement which is tax free.

One area which is fun is equities and investing in such asset-backed investments. Depending on your willingness to take the time and make the effort, you can open up a whole new world of investigation from which you can develop new skills and new experiences – and profit from this knowledge. The downside is you do need more skills and more knowledge and these take up an inordinate amount of time. You may wish to engage the services of a professional trusted adviser to carry these out on your behalf.

This is an area where you can design your own portfolio to deliver your desired lifestyle and work/life balance, which maximises an effective and efficient portfolio construction at work, and a most meaningful life outside work.

Venture capital trusts and enterprise investment schemes offer 30% tax relief and tax-free income and opportunities to become more widely diversified and involved in your investments. Each of these has attractive advantages alongside risk, restrictions and disadvantages. Some of the disadvantages are your money is tied up in a contract for five years. You are invested in stocks and shares with more risks attached, and these have to be balanced against the advantage of the tax relief, and tax-free income and potential for capital growth.

All these savings and investment schemes can take up a lot of time and require a depth of knowledge with which you may not wish to engage or get involved. Each investment can assist you to reach your desired goals and aspirations but they require constant monitoring and significant losses can also be racked up.

Some of the major disadvantages are the complex arrangements and sales strategies using jargon acronyms, and the charges applied. Each institution has its own jargon for what is basically the same charge. For example, there are some 40 different names for charges in mortgages – used effectively to complicate and confuse the end user i.e. you the customer. Why do they need to do that? Why do they not have one set of terms for each charge? A cynical person might assume this is to ensure your need to compare products and services is made as difficult as possible to remove their competition, and by activating such a strategy many people are misled, and accept a product.

Each of these types of investment can be arranged with a view to educating your children, or for providing you with a fund of money to be used throughout your retirement. They can be used for tax-efficient investing but can also be adapted to be used for paying for school fees or further education at university. However, you should be aware they are set up for reducing tax primarily. Educational fees would need to be arranged alongside your salary or other high-interest savings and deposit accounts where the savings cannot go down. Put simply, a two-year term in cash or low-risk investments – to ensure payment and to make an allowance for any volatility in markets – means you have set aside the funds and have peace of mind the cash will be available. This strategy may be at the expense of increases in the markets, or reductions in the markets.

When planning family finances a Junior ISA is available to UK resident children under age 18 who do not have a child trust fund account, or to children from 6 April 2015 for those who wish to transfer a Child Trust Fund to a Junior ISA. The maximum amount is £4,080 for 2105/2016 .

This can be an effective and efficient way to transfer assets down through the family. After the age of 18 these children have full access to these funds, and loss of control may be an issue.

Cash held in Individual Savings Accounts (ISA's) used to permit a deposit up to £5,348 and these may be used to provide tax-free interest and tax-free growth or tax-free income. Changes to legislation, now allow the full £25,240 to be deposited for 2015/2016 tax year. However, given the interest rates available and the fact that there is no capital gains tax on NISA's it would be bizarre to use a NISA in the form of a deposit account rather than exploit the valuable other benefits available. These need to be more fully explained to clients i.e. using the right products for the correct solutions

This is another area where money is only a means of keeping count. Such investing makes you establish how much you will need and when you will need it. Inflation and the amount you will need to save can be calculated using simple sums, and investments cashed in when school fees become payable before each term.

Having fun with your money can mean investing or purchasing alternative investments or other external products, such as creating a garden, conservatory or summer house. This can give you an immeasurable amount of pleasure. Investing in gold, coins, art, metal or other alternative investments all require more in-depth investigation, and such specialist products can be very time consuming and more volatile.

CHAPTER 9:
How to find your trusted financial planner

From a financial planner's point of view it is essential to build up a professional business practice using a sound business model.

In the past advisers have relied on insurance companies and investment houses paying them large amounts of upfront commission which may seem at first generous, depending on the type of business, e.g. endowments, pensions, or life assurance policies paying commissions in percentage terms, directly linked to your annual premiums. In sales managers' jargon, these advisers are often referred to as "hunter gatherers", and that "they eat what they kill".

The adviser's remuneration may be taken from upfront commissions in percentage terms from the total contributions made, e.g. in pensions where basic rate tax is added to your premium, and commissions are paid to the adviser based on the gross amount invested, plus an annual percentage on the value of your portfolio.

This business model requires the salesperson to find a constant supply of new customers, which may have the effect of reducing the ongoing services. One of the issues with commissions is if you pay upfront commissions or fees you lose control of the service. Paying on a more regular, open and transparent basis should remedy such poor service standards, although there is no guarantee. Fees which are transparent and explained upfront for the services agreed prior to planning or investing, or purchasing any product or service, is the way forward. Such a clear and open business model removes doubt and is precise in the service and standards and increases trust. Other professional organisations operate such a service.

An adviser needs to build up a solid picture of your income and expenditure, your assets and liabilities, your willingness to establish your goals, your needs and your willingness to implement their advice. If you fail to implement their advice you are wasting your time and the time of your adviser. An adviser needs to be fully acquainted of your attitude and willingness to taking risk, and apply this to your specific portfolio. A good adviser will already have experience in this area and assist you to avoid some of the pitfalls and help you decide the most suitable products designed to meet your specific lifestyle.

With a sound professional process in place it is essential to gather all the relevant information prior to taking any decision on strategy, or investing, or prior to purchasing a product. In my opinion, people should avoid direct salespeople and those flogging products – especially banks – where banks have no interest in you as a long-term customer, only as a one-off hit profit centre flogging their product to you. How any product purchased fits in with your financial plan is for you to decide.

However, for our Lifesmart® Financial Planners Ltd customer, it makes sense to plan for the type and quality of advice you require. Before looking to engage an adviser, it is essential to look at the type of service you require, along with the level of service you require, and for the most suitable advice. We refer to this as 'value': the value an adviser can bring to your finances, your lifestyle, and the important independent and unbiased advice as your agent, and the research team.

Start by looking at the level and complexity of the service you require. For example, many people may only be looking for a transactional service such as a mortgage or a pension plan. Others may be looking at tax efficiency or wealth management, or specific advice on a particular area such as retirement planning or estate planning. Be prepared to pay for the advice if you want independent and unbiased advice.

So where can you obtain advice?

Financial advice is available from many sources and the quality and quantity varies dramatically. The advice provided from the following requires you, the individual, to conduct various levels of work and research and to take full responsibility for the choice of product and funds etc.

Different levels of advice and different levels of service may be obtained from the following:

- Do it yourself (DIY)

- General newspapers, reports, the internet, tip sheets and libraries

- Banks, building societies and the Post Office

- Restricted advisers or company representatives, tied agents and multi-tied agents

- Independent Financial Advisers – independent or restricted

- Independent financial planners – independent and unbiased

Each of these areas of advice offers different levels of service which require different levels of knowledge, different levels of skill and the onus is on each individual (i.e. you) to take different levels of responsibility.

Tied agents or independent advice?

When I joined the insurance industry in 1979, and until more recently, there were only two types of advice: independent advice from insurance brokers and the restricted advice of the company-tied agents.

Both agents were remunerated by commissions from product providers in the main. However, the main legal difference is the Independent Financial Adviser was the agent of the individual and has certain specific duties and due diligence under law, whereas the tied agent was the agent of the product provider (under their master and servant relationship).

Nowadays the whole issue of advice has become much more complicated, with a myriad of remuneration systems which may not necessarily be better and is often less clear or transparent. HMRC requires VAT to be added to an invoice/fee for 'advice'. VAT does not apply to commissions. As a consequence, some advisers complicate the issue by claiming in the way of a fee which is taken by way of a percentage of the fund, paid for by the product provider – which is in effect commissions.

However, a more structured approach has been introduced which offers the opportunity to be more open and transparent. I believe this allows for a more meaningful engagement and discussion. More information is available on the internet which has educated many, which is good, but it has also meant information overload. I believe the internet, whilst developing a marketplace which has complicated and diluted the value of advice and the provision of advice, ignores many of the areas such as tax and the removal of setting your long-term goals.

Using the internet services

With benefits from the internet comes the do-it-yourself customer. There have always been those who feel they can do it themselves without help or intervention and who embrace many new ideas or services. Cost is usually claimed to be the biggest factor and the driving force. However, to identify the loss of good sound advice may mean lower investment returns or poor product choice. We look to a cost benefit analysis. Those who feel they have the knowledge, the skill and who read widely and may be influenced by a newspaper article or internet comment may have the inherent belief that they have sufficient knowledge and/or the ability to carry out such professional services. Students of finance have spent years, or in some cases decades, in ongoing learning. There can be no compensation for the education, the skill and experience learned over the years.

We now live in a society where some people believe they can turn on an adviser or their product provider to make a claim when something has not worked out, for whatever reason. Their objective is to recoup the cost of failing to conduct due diligence and effectively claim for compensation or damages when things do not work out, or if truly misled, e.g. mis-selling. Failure of people to read the contract terms or conduct in-depth research and the lack of understanding on how insurance companies work are the main areas which cause product providers concern.

Problems have arisen because some people purchase contracts on the basis of sales and marketing adverts without conducting due diligence and the old favourite of *caveat emptor* (let the buyer beware) applies.

Problems from this type of activity are on the increase by more sneaky advertising and appear to be causing more issues and complaints as a result of uncontrolled, improper or misleading promotions. Poor communication results in poor service from product providers, along with untrained employees and a failure to correct complaints, errors and so on. Such inherent company failures in these activities place more work on product providers, and they withdraw and withhold assistance on the basis of no one will take responsibility and that there may be a complaint – causing even more unnecessary and unpleasant work for employees, more anxiety for customers, frustration and increasing the cost of products.

Those who are buying products and services direct must realise they are buying products based on their own knowledge and skill – and they must take full responsibility for their actions. Secondly, the impact on these purchases means product providers have to be alert to those buying products online, which may change their minds, with a sudden outflow of cash for the provider.

Put simply, these short-term activities distort the marketplace, which adds further volatility. As a result, product providers, in an attempt to reduce costs, make their employees redundant – often the most expensive, the most experienced and the employees with the best knowledge. Outsourcing work to the Far East or India leaves UK companies compromised and losing the training and competence of middle management. Their ability goes first as they are the highest cost and will find other employment. The companies are then left with the remnants of their workforce, which reduces services further.

The press and journalists

Product providers are often the source of information and a starting point for financial reporters and newspaper journalists. Financial advice is available in the press in abundance. National and local newspapers are provided with the sales pitches of product providers who turn them into stories, usually on one particular aspect, designed to sell newspapers rather than provide good all-round sound financial planning advice. The disadvantage of using this medium is it is based only on one particular aspect or product, which may be restricted to a few column inches and which is flavour of the month, e.g. pensions, mortgages or investments, to get their headline rate in. This is often at the expense of pointing out the disadvantages. The reason behind this is the editor's desire to promote some of the features at the expense of others. However, as with any form of propaganda or sales literature, the devil is always in the detail.

To save time, effort and money it is extremely important that you read the detail e.g. the contract terms.

Financial planning, however, is used to demonstrate how each area of your finances works, and how they interact and impact on the other areas of your finances. You only need to look back through press reports on the benefits of mortgage endowments – and in later years when the press turned and was extremely harsh highlighting the disadvantages of the products they were so supportive of in years prior. Put simply, the press are followers of fashionable products and in an effort to sell newspapers and attract advertising introduce bias, missing many informative points.

Which? reports and financial advice offers an independent source – but once again restricted to specific products or specific areas rather than good, sound, all-round advice. It seems many of the practical issues are left out. *Which?* reports have a tendency to come up with some form of comparison based on specific requirements, but as a result of this, and their desire to encompass all their readers, has limitations. It is useful background reading but as space is limited it is a generalisation and makes much information available not as comprehensive or client specific as it might otherwise be.

Bank employees as advisers and tied agents

Similarly, financial advice is available from financial institutions such as banks, building societies, the Post Office or National Savings, and more latterly supermarkets. Such advice relies on the sale of products rather than the provision of financial planning advice and these product-selling institutions are rewarded for their sales through the payment of commissions. These can vary widely and often the charges go unchallenged and are in general accepted. As a result, charges may be higher than elsewhere, e.g. banks have their captive market, their client banks. We often see different departments of banks offering different levels of interest or service, sometimes acting directly opposite their colleagues. This is due to lack of coordination and communication.

Financial advice is available from company-sponsored salespeople referred to in law as tied agents, who represent their sponsoring company, selling only their products. Once again, rewarded by commissions they are tied to their company by only being permitted to sell the products of their sponsoring company. In return for commissions the sponsoring company has to provide them with authorisation, some level of training, and the level of support will be determined by how committed to the provision of financial services the sponsoring company is. The company adviser may be rewarded by a basic salary and bonus or commissions or be more fully employed. Whichever way the adviser is rewarded, they need to meet specific targets, which bear no relation to what the customer may require.

Another form of tied agent is the multi-tied agent, so called because they have tied agency agreements with more than one company, whilst operating under the umbrella of their master company, their sponsor or principal. As a result, they may be able to offer the products or services of more than one company or fund, with more than one charging structure and different commission terms available. One such example of a multi-tied agency is St James's Place.

The main difference from a tied agent or multi-tied agent is they are the representative of their sponsoring company or multiple companies, who are driven by targets and sales and who look for clients to fit their products rather than products or services to fit the customer's needs.

The Independent Financial Adviser

Financial advice is also available from Independent Financial Advisers or IFAs as they are often referred to. Independent Financial Advisers can offer products and services from the whole of market, or from a restricted range, hence the term "restricted adviser". More recently the Financial Conduct Authority (FCA) introduced changes to their legislation which state that Independent Financial Advisers must offer clients the opportunity to be remunerated for the work involved by way of a fee, or they may take commissions or they may offset commissions against their fees.

One problem for clients who pay out of their funds is they are taken from tax efficient investments usually producing a further drag on their investments. Some clients lose the facility to offset charges against their tax assessment, to further reduce their tax liability.

Some Independent Financial Advisers offer a transactional service and continue to take commissions rather than fees. Often this is to protect themselves against the work involved, and the early termination of a contract by a client who might be fickle, or untrustworthy, and not instil trust. Most reasonable IFAs are looking to develop a long-term business relationship. Some clients may only wish to seek out information and use their IFA for their knowledge and skill on a small point or area of business. Some clients may then go direct to the insurance company without realising the commissions are still being taken out of their product – but these commissions remain with the insurance company to cross-subsidise other areas or loss leaders. I enjoyed many a client purchasing products direct during my time at Scottish Widows where I was remunerated for no work involved – and in my opinion the adviser and client still lost out massively. This is one good reason why an independent adviser will agree the fees **prior** to carrying out any work. During this time some consultants who passed business to their team or business produced IFAs by way of an inducement, who received the commissions but the client was unaware they had been placed with an IFA. These inducements for business may have become more difficult under the FCA and regulators.

When an IFA (or company representative or tied agent) conducts work on behalf of a client it means they should be remunerated for the work carried out – whether by way of commissions or bonus and where, if a client terminates the contract early, the client can lose out financially. I was notified by Scottish Widows as a broker consultant/inspector of clients who terminated business with their IFA and applied directly to

Scottish Widows afterwards successfully, to the financial detriment of the IFA. As a broker consultant I was rewarded with the bonus for new business from wherever it arose. In my opinion, this was a conflict of interest and it was, and may still be as far as I am aware, company policy. Claims of poor record keeping are not acceptable excuses – but it helps the company.

The process of financial planning

Professional financial planners offer a service of financial planning advice which looks at the assets and liabilities of a client, the income and expenditure, and developing a financial plan. A financial planning model based on the client's cash flow, to ensure it is suitable and affordable now and for the future and designed to meet a client's objectives. This is referred to as cash flow modelling.

Such a lifetime cash flow model is essential and demonstrates a client can afford the recommendations, and the plan all adds up going forward. A good lifetime cash flow model can demonstrate the various 'what if' scenarios which may have a catastrophic effect on their finances. Alternatively, a client may for instance inherit money, sell a property, wish to downsize or implement their pension fund, or take income in the most tax-efficient manner or the fund is increased or reduced for whatever reason. Each of these may be quite common and they have to be built into any worthwhile and competent written financial plan.

In this book we are looking at couples and families in the middle of their careers. We are looking towards couples with their children who have become financially independent and they are building their wealth and reducing their tax to provide for themselves as they approach retirement. Whilst increasing their wealth or reducing their tax, the protection of their assets is often ignored or their focus is diverted.

Decide on your priorities. Assess your willingness to take risk and the economic climate which could damage your strategy. There is no need to take additional risks, when the result of risk does not provide any significant improvement in your returns. Decide on what you want to achieve. Once these have been recognised you look at your income and your expenditure, apply your assumptions and develop a lifetime cash flow. Decisions on savings and decisions on how best to invest may then be considered.

CASE STUDY

Doing nothing can sometimes be good advice

We had a client who came to us with £65,000 in a with–profits policy and had been advised to switch to another company by his adviser. As he was concerned he wanted a second opinion. The surrender or transfer value charge from the insurance company was £2,000 and the charge for advice i.e. commissions was £3,000. Our advice was the client had five years to the selected retirement age and we felt it would be very difficult to build up £5,000 in growth from the fund in the prevailing climate, and switching from a with–profits to a unit-linked product which is more directly linked to the stock market, which is volatile, might be dangerous to his pension portfolio.

As it turned out, the following year stock markets fell and our monitoring showed our client his fund would have been worth £47,000 after charges, commissions and losses. His fund had not been affected as he took our advice and as the pension fund was held in with–profits and protected against the ravages of the stock market because of the smoothing process. The client had paid us for our recommendations, rather than opt for commissions which required the sale of a product – and a year and a half further on his fund was valued at £83,000.

Since then the client has just retired with a fund of £123,000. Had he taken the 'advice' route his fund would be worth £97,300 – a difference of £25,700. The only person who can confirm our remuneration was good value for money is the client. The main benefit in my opinion was the peace of mind from the point of our advice to the date selected to take the fund, and the constant monitoring and updating of the fund.

Good advice is worth paying for. We continue to monitor the investment and we are switching out of equities and into gilts and fixed interest, and with another year to go the client has the peace of mind knowing we are looking after him and trusted to look after his retirement fund. This client is self-employed and we suggested he look to ISA investments (cash and equity) to provide additional security and access to funds, if required. It is all about what you want to achieve – your objectives.

When the client reached 65 years of age, he returned to request more information on how he could best utilise his fund. Our request to the insurance company showed his fund to be valued at £123,000 with options for a tax-free lump sum of 25% of the fund plus an annuity, or a higher level of annuity. We pointed out that by using the open market option under his policy contract terms he could obtain a higher level of annuity (see Glossary). We also pointed out that as a result of health issues he could obtain an even higher rate of annuity – an increase of some 40%.

Total return

It is at times like these when total return brings about real worth. Each year we look at a client's portfolios and check the charges against the investment returns, against the previous year, to calculate total return for the client.

How to calculate total return

Check

To assess the value for money you can do this through calculating your total return. To do this you need to establish your investment return and divide this by the amount you have invested plus the fees and charges, as in the following formula:

$$\text{Total return} = \frac{(P_1 - P_0) + D}{P_0}$$

Where P1 is initial price (to include increments less charges and fees)
Po is end price
D is dividends

Notes: An increased annuity for poor health means the insurance company has calculated the client has a restricted term of life, which in some clients might cause anxiety, concerns or depression.

I am no particular fan of with–profits products due to their complex nature, opaque charging structure and their manipulation by the product provider, but there are times when these products have merit, and this is an example of when emotions have to be removed from your finances, and products used which are practical.

CHAPTER 10:
The Lifesmart financial planning strategy and process

The benefits of financial planning are clearly set out upfront. Your objectives are clear and you agree your decision on direction and strategy, as a result of the trust built up in the knowledge you are being looked after over your lifetime. This enables you to control your finances, and examine and analyse your financial affairs to ensure you get what you want from the service, with sound professional and ethical advice. Financial planning is about ensuring you do not run out of money during your life, it allows you to enjoy the lifestyle you want to achieve and meet the goals you have set for yourself.

Most important of all, it gives you direction and control along with meaning and brings reason to your financial decisions. In addition to this, it provides you with a check and monitoring process with expert unbiased advice.

During your lifetime you will meet challenges and changes; consideration of these needs to be addressed proactively by planning, concepts, ideas and solutions as to how you might deal with them. Each individual's circumstances are unique and any written financial plan should reflect these differences, and the client's needs.

Personal financial planning: its meaning and its purpose

There are many definitions, from ensuring you never run out of money to much longer comprehensive paragraphs to cover every possible aspect. Financial planning can be implemented for individuals, couples or business owners and for business succession.

My definition of financial planning is:

The establishment and development of a comprehensive financial plan that is tailored to an individual's or couple's needs, which maximises and protects financial resources, and is adapted to meet ever-changing circumstances during the various stages of his or her life.

Most people choose advice for the complex issues around pensions, Inheritance Tax planning and areas of investing. Many advisers use these as part of their armoury of sales pitches – from point of contact to the direct sales process, what used to be referred to as 'reversing the hearse up to the door and letting them smell the flowers'. Fear selling is not new. However, fear selling is a product of contract flogging – usually to get a point across from a salesperson who is unable to argue their point or is more engaged with a prospect to influence the sale, in return for the commissions the product will generate rather than provide the client with benefits.

The most successful method of planning your finances for couples and everybody else is:

- Set measureable goals

- Develop an understanding of how the impact of one financial decision will impact on other areas of finance

- Continuous monitoring and re-evaluation of your lifetime cash flow – your financial plan

- Start with where you are now (be brutal, be accurate)

- Look at the overall picture of your finances

- Do not wait until there is a crisis (family or finance)

- Analyse, research and back test them

- Make a decision: Act – do it now!

As an independent financial planner we look to working with you, building up a rapport and trust. It is important for us to gather all the relevant information on your circumstances, to build up the bigger overall picture, and help you to prioritise and get financially well organised. Unfortunately this can be tedious, but it is absolutely necessary. It may feel like a police interrogation rather than the basis for your financial planning. It has to be effortless and engaging, and most of all enjoyable and worthwhile.

We need to define our role and the relationship we have, and then document the services to be provided and how decisions will be made. From a background of direct sales and then broker sales before becoming an Independent Financial Adviser (IFA) for a national broker at the British Medical Association Services Ltd (BMA Services Ltd), specifically for the NHS, doctors and dentists, I found this to be the hardest part of my work. Our fact finding process had to be quick, and it felt more like an interrogation before we could deliver our advice. Truth be known, we knew what we were going to sell before we met a client. Being used to selling products and being remunerated by way of commissions meant I was working for the insurance company or product provider, rather than my client or myself.

When using an adviser, the relationship has to be agreed at the outset, including the remuneration (the fee agreement) before conducting any work. The terms of business and terms of engagement must be fully agreed and the remuneration clearly explained. Once the adviser and client have agreed these the relationship is established and together you can move forward and engage on the next stage and gather all the relevant information before establishing your lifetime cash flow (Lifesmart® Financial Plan).

Before starting on your financial plan, it seems basic but you need to decide precisely what you want to achieve. Decisions, decisions, decisions! But prioritised and taken in order brings with it organisation, removal of prevarication and confidence that you are doing the right thing.

Other external factors need to be considered such as the cost of eating out. Do you want a few drinks or to join clubs?

Once you decide on your objectives, your desired lifestyle, you can move effortlessly to the next stage.

Many banks and insurance companies use the example of 'the journey' to sell their products along the way. However, a financial plan is more than just a journey, it is a lifestyle experience modelled around your situation, designed to meet your needs and your requirements.

I had the greatest pleasure of watching an expert locksmith at work. It was truly amazing to see him look at the lock, and cleverly move the tools of his trade around inside with expert skill and knowledge to use his craft to make the internal mechanism of the lock operate effectively and efficiently.

Selling the service

Another example of planning is watching the craft of a pilot. We climb on board the plane and expect it to take off and land as confirmed but the work behind the scenes is enormous. It begins with the engineering of the aircraft and its constant maintenance and fit for purpose tests. The ongoing training of employees in all aspects of the aircraft continues with the training of employees on the ground and in the hangers. The training carried on to supplement service and give the passenger a great experience, or in the case of the low-budget airlines an experience they are unlikely to complain about due to cheap flights. All the training of cabin crew and everyone associated means working together to provide you with the all-round airline experience. The many hours of training which go into the set routine we all need to listen to before take-off. There are good reasons for this. It is all about safety! It is all about confidence!

The pilots start with a thorough knowledge of their aircraft, the airport and the requirements to obey those in the tower who are aware of what is all around, the bigger picture, and are controlling many other aircraft, e.g. Heathrow has a flight going in or out every two or three minutes. Before the pilot climbs aboard, the captain and his crew have pre-flight checks on the aircraft itself. Fuel levels, wind and weather conditions along the route, and more routine checks by the pilot and co-pilot for passenger safety. The flight plan is organised in advance, and the route provided which is flexible enough that changes can be made if necessary. All this work prior to a flight – all behind the scenes, it does not just happen, and so it is with financial planning.

Preparing for financial planning and creating your lifetime cash flow is just as onerous. Why would you request any bank employee to conduct complicated calculations to take in external factors such as inflation, external economic conditions in the UK or elsewhere? The journey often conveyed by product providers is their strategy designed to sell a product which may be suitable and which may also be expensive. It is important to decide on the level of risk to take and assess if your needs can be met by taking less risk. Many product providers bundle together several products to increase their product sales, often with reduced contract terms or contract restrictions.

The level of risk for different needs may well vary. For example, the level of risk you are willing to take to pay off a small debt will be different from that of a much larger sum. You may feel you have to be more cautious given the large amount, but depending on the term, you might be able to take a higher level of risk. It is important to look at the bigger picture.

Responsibility

Before setting out on the financial planning process any adviser needs to ensure their clients are fully aware of their responsibilities before they conduct any work. These responsibilities are:

1. You will be responsible for the reliability, accuracy and completeness of the information you provide.

2. You have undertaken to make available to us, as and when required, all the financial information required and related information, including minutes of management meetings, necessary to carry out our work.

Scope of our work

Once we have all the relevant information, we confirm with our clients the scope of the work to be undertaken. Where information has not been provided we would confirm the basis on which we are to be engaged in this area, and of our service standards. Where necessary, if there are areas where no information or little information is provided and we could not give any assurances to the reasonableness or accuracy of the information or records, we would confirm whether we could provide the report from the records as being a true and fair view.

Once we have gathered all the relevant information, agreed the client's objectives, assessed the risk profile of each client and established their priorities, we move to the next stage of analysing and evaluating the various alternatives. This includes looking at external influences such as inflation, and build this into our lifetime cash flow model. For example, RPI inflation may be around 0.5% but your personal inflation may be 5.2% built on your basket of items, e.g. mortgage, electricity etc. Inflation on individual items such as energy (gas and electricity) may be higher and any one client may use more of that particular item. When considering options the model must be allowed to calculate 'what if' scenarios to allow building into the model your personal inflation in order for you to identify and make considered judgments.

Do not use RPI or CPI in your personal calculations; decide on your own personal inflation and monitor it each year until it becomes a habit.

When we are building a plan we need to look at and agree each of the assumptions against the market, using the Office of National Statistics (ONS) or other national figures to ensure you feel comfortable with them. This includes the level of risk you are willing to take for the return you require. We look at inflation, the asset allocation, diversification, the costs and any taxation involved to estimate your chances of success. With the correct assumptions in place the requirements need to meet your needs; the necessary requirements to meet your objectives cannot be argued.

One of the key aspects of a financial planner is ethical behaviour. This includes clearing up misunderstandings, and dealing with complaints effectively, efficiently and professionally. This should be carried out by the directors taking their duties and responsibilities seriously. It is the behaviour in these financial institutions which needs to be addressed by the companies themselves and if not, by the regulator, the FCA.

Behaviour, integrity, knowledge and competence of any individual or firm are of the highest importance.

Integrity without knowledge is weak and useless, and knowledge without integrity is dangerous and dreadful.

SAMUEL JOHNSON

The Lifesmart® Financial Plan

Once we have developed the financial plan, which has to be in writing and addresses our Lifesmart® lifetime cash flow model, it is prepared and designed to meet your desired lifestyle. It must then be implemented, and we confirm a date by which this needs to be carried out. Confirming the dates when our work must be completed is good efficient planning for our practice, and setting target dates by which clients must fulfil their responsibilities should help to prevent prevarication. This process then sets the strategy which, when implemented in an efficient and effective manner and for the benefit of all, should meet the desired outcomes. These efficiencies need to be relayed to our clients by way of effective and efficient management which inspires trust in our practice. It also means we can keep costs down by having our Lifesmart® processes in place. By having a set process it has the added benefit for our practice of cutting out wasted time which is costly and which often creates additional and unnecessary work for everyone involved.

Once the financial plan has been designed and agreed it simply must be implemented!

From then on the Lifesmart® Financial Plan needs regular ongoing monitoring, the recommendations regularly reviewed at our annual meeting, and we need to ensure we continue to work within the scope of the work requested. Sometimes just a few tweaks are needed to keep the plan on course, or if significant changes are required, a more in-depth knowledge and assessment needs to be carried out.

The results are reviewed and recommendations challenged each year, as an integral part of our contract terms. This provides for an ongoing business relationship and creates peace of mind for clients to know we are only a telephone call away and that each year they will review our efforts and advise if there are any necessary changes. Being Lifesmart® is all about planning for a lifestyle – not about flogging products.

Our processes and financial planning systems allow us to monitor how much time is spent by each employee, the complexity of work carried out, the checks and balances and compliances along with any delays, prevarications or disruption and poor quality service from product providers. Each has a financial cost, and so can be identified and charged out accordingly to the appropriate company.

A client can if they wish keep costs to a minimum by providing all the relevant information in a timely manner. If not, an adviser reserves the right to charge an additional fee for any extra or unnecessary work created or further work needed to complete the exercise. Accuracy of information is crucial if the recommendations are to stand up to scrutiny, and whilst errors and omissions will continue to exist, they can be caught early or noticed to prevent an issue developing and causing hassle further down the line.

For any client it is the total return which is most appealing. Total return is the profit made from the original point to the amount at the point of checking, after taking into account all charges and any increments.

CHAPTER 11:
Planning for a catastrophe

Nothing in life is certain except death and taxes.

This rather fatalistic and sardonic proverb draws on the inevitability of death. Statistics of death since time immemorial remain to this day to be one in one. The taxes, originally to raise money for the war chests of previous kings to invade and plunder but which now appear as a burden to us all, also remain. As society becomes more complex the taxes required become a greater burden on society – and sometimes not distributed as evenly as we might like.

Several authors have used these lines to good effect, but it was Daniel Defoe in *The Political History of The Devil* in 1726 who first used the line:

Things as certain as death and taxes can be more firmly believed.

Benjamin Franklyn (1706-1790) used the form we are more familiar with in a letter to Jean-Baptiste Leroy (1789) which was printed in *The Works of Benjamin Franklyn, 1817*:

In this world nothing can be said to be certain, except death and taxes.

Many salespeople have used these as throwaway lines to point out the certainty of death and to raise the awareness of taxes, designed to instigate and generate anxiety and concerns for the opportunity for selling protection policies or reducing tax – looking to their commissions rather than the real benefits of protection policies. Good financial planners look to their clients' needs uppermost. I refer to this as being 'service above self'.

As we travel through life from childhood and puberty, various stages of working and into retirement we are taxed against our income. Capital Gains Tax is applied to our investments and, through indirect taxes such as National Insurance, VAT, car tax, TV licence etc., on towards death and Inheritance Tax (IHT, the only tax which is voluntary). One wag once said IHT is the only tax where people would prefer to pay the taxman than give to their children or next of kin. Put simply, prefers the taxman to their family!

In passing on your wealth to your heirs and beneficiaries, it is important to have a valid Will. A Will gives direction to who you wish to receive your assets, whether in money, gifts or assets. If you do not have a valid Will there can be no disposition of your estate. As a consequence you are considered to have died intestate. The courts will decide on the distribution of your estate. A partial intestacy occurs where there is an incomplete disposition of an estate.

Unfortunately, over the decades of decay in the insurance industry, the overselling of policies to meet targets and commissions has replaced many of the benefits provided. Many of the insurance policies derided in the national press and the advisers demonised due to their reliance on product provider's information have been reduced to their basic level. This is mainly due to the lack of education and lack of training by the employers of tied agents and direct salesforces and product-flogging salespeople who are expendable if they do not meet these unrealistic targets.

But death is a serious business and a whole industry relies on it, from Will drafters, to funeral directors, limousine companies and crematoriums. Now the cost of funerals is increasing dramatically and can be in excess of £5,000. Have you prepared for this cost?

The most serious catastrophe is for the family of loved ones, or the business owners and their marriage partners of company directors or partnerships. Usually one person is the breadwinner in the household or in the business. The loss of those earnings can be catastrophic financially and emotionally and may have disastrous effects on families and on the remaining directors of the business or partnership.

Have you made a Business Will?

The importance of a Will cannot be stressed enough. Your Will gives formal written direction of your wishes to your executors, and for those you wish to benefit.

Business owners should also have a Business Will, a predetermined strategy to allow fellow directors and partners in business, and their partner in life, not to lose out on your hard work. By setting up a Business Will your fellow director or business partner has reassurance and security of knowing they will not end up with their ex-director's spouse's next partner as their partner in business.

The business can continue in the way it was intended without external interference or disturbance and, if correctly made, with sufficient funds to ensure continuity of the business.

The death or long-term sickness of a business partner or fellow director can cause many problems such as having to find and pay for someone to take over their job, usually at a higher cost than the key man or key woman, and who is likely to be less committed.

A 'key person' is someone who may have invested money in the business, or be a key employee who may be difficult or expensive to replace. In the event of untimely death or long-term illness it makes sense to have in place financial provision for such a catastrophe. Simple financial planning using the appropriate product can provide a lump sum of cash or ongoing payments when your key employee is off sick.

> Term assurance policies or sickness and accident policies such as permanent health insurance (PHI) whilst providing a potentially useful product, need due diligence to be carried out on the company's claims procedures and actual pay outs. This also provides additional confidence in such a tardy industry and demonstrates the quality of the company chosen at the outset and their dealings with the claim. Only after conducting such work can clients have peace of mind.

One way in order to protect the business owner and key individuals against premature death or sickness and accident is to outsource the risk. Purchasing a life assurance policy with a sum assured that pays out on death or on a critical illness is one way of providing such a lump sum, in a simple way. The amount required will depend on the regular outgoings of family life, adding on any debts. For example, with the loss of a family member, using a figure of 5% return on the lump sum means you are looking to protect the capital amount whilst giving the family the interest or the yield to live on and giving some protection to the capital sum. If capital is required at a later stage you can look towards using some of the capital sum – for example when a family is grown up, mortgage debts repaid etc. Using the cash flow model, such capital payments mean a greater understanding of the effects this will have. Can you afford to take a larger amount than the recommended amount from your portfolio? If you do, you are at risk of reducing the capital.

If someone in the family is unable to work through sickness or accident this too becomes a catastrophe which can be catered for through careful financial planning. Product providers offer two different types of policy:

1. Sickness and accident

2. Permanent health insurance (PHI)

Both products offer the opportunity to protect your income – usually between 50% and may be up to 75%. The maximum amount is set by the product provider to give some encouragement to return to work at the earliest time. This also has the effect of keeping premiums down.

The main difference between sickness and accident policies and permanent health insurance is sickness and accident policies may be payable for 12 months normally and reviewed yearly, and the offer to renew comes from the product provider. Permanent health insurance is permanent in that you select a retirement date and then, provided you continue paying the premiums and meet the product terms, the contract cannot be terminated by the product provider, on the proviso you have met the product provider's terms and conditions.

However, as you grow older your body starts to suffer from wear and tear and your health may deteriorate. Premiums are assessed on the risks and older ages mean premiums become more expensive. Ill health may also affect the premiums and in some cases may be refused by insurers as the risk is too high. This is a reason why it is important to select the right product as early as possible and use the product to its full advantage throughout your life.

A good example of this is the difference between permanent life assurance i.e. whole of life assurance, in comparison to term assurance i.e. temporary assurance. Protection against death is called 'assurance' whereas protection of property (assets such as buildings and contents or motoring cover) is called 'insurance'.

The purchase of a whole of life policy means a lump sum of money will be provided to the beneficiary or to the family for the whole of your life (provided premiums are maintained) in the event of death. The sum assured pays out directly to the family if written correctly and without

IHT liability to allow the family to continue with the lifestyle they had originally planned. Put simply, to protect the family life and the desired lifestyle attained. The sum assured obviously cannot replace the person yet it is designed to alleviate the financial burden. Overcoming the emotions during these times of grieving, the life assurance policy is designed to remove at least the financial strain.

One simple proposition is to take out a whole of life policy for an agreed sum assured and use the policy for protection in the early years while continuing with paying premiums, and on death the sum assured is paid out to your family. If arranged alongside a suitable trust fund, the sum assured will be outside your estate, and therefore tax free to your beneficiaries. If your children are not yet 18, the trustees are charged with looking after the funds until the children reach 18 or the age required and set by the trust.

Clearly large amounts of cash create their own problems, e.g. tax and where to invest, but these can be reduced by taking your own decisions or employing your trusted adviser.

On top of the life assurance you can add the opportunity to increase the level of protection in line with the RPI or as a percentage of the original sum assured. These guaranteed insurability clauses help to provide additional protection at some point in later life when the body starts to wear out and protection at normal rates might be more difficult to obtain. But beware, commission at the full rate is applied to these premiums for advisers. This does not detract from the benefit conferred, but is often omitted during a product sale.

Another add on which I select for many clients, especially those who are self-employed, is waiver of premium – which means if you are off sick through illness and accident the insurer will pay the premium on your behalf until you are able to return to work.

With all these products it is essential you take full responsibility and read the product terms.

CASE STUDY

We had a client who was off sick for over a year, his policy was set up to protect his family. They had a mortgage and the family had increased their mortgage because of having more children. He had good earnings but was injured in a car crash. The insurance company paid his premium because he had waiver of premium included in his policy and the family were extremely grateful because money was tight. They had an extra mouth to feed and his wife had to keep going back to the hospital until he recovered sufficiently. This benefit meant they continued to keep the life assurance protection, throughout illness, without worry. They had originally called me in to confirm they could not keep the policy going as finances were tight. They thanked me for insisting on adding waiver of premium to their policy and it was a moment of warmth when they said, "You do not realise how valuable this life assurance is until you might need it." Thankfully in this case the husband recovered and went back to work 19 months after the accident.

He telephoned me later to thank me and tell me he was back at work. He then sent me a lovely letter saying how valuable his life assurance policy was to him, knowing his family would be looked after financially if he had died. He also said that had it not been for the waiver of premium they would probably not have been able to keep up the payments and the protection would have lapsed.

These are the benefits of a good insurance policy: to meet financial commitments and standards of living in times of untimely ill health or death.

CASE STUDY

We had a young couple where the husband had come out of the army, set up in business as a sole trader and they had two young daughters. Business was doing well and we were asked to quote for life assurance and critical illness. His bank manager had been in touch to set up a policy which he felt was very expensive. We offered much more protection at a lower premium and with more benefits at a figure of £306,250 for £100 per month (including waiver of premium and guaranteed insurability). The bank offered £65,000 for £80 per month subject to their underwriting requirements.

Interestingly, the sum assured only covered the bank overdraft amount and took no account of the family protection needs. Needing the overdraft and the continuous pressure and basically bullying and threats of removal of the overdraft facility by the bank salesman, he agreed to £245,000 of life assurance and critical illness cover from us through Scottish Provident for a premium of £80 per month. He agreed to take £50,000 life assurance and critical illness cover (no waiver of premium) for £40 per month through another Scottish insurance company. He met all the underwriting stipulations answering all the medical questions and sailed through Scottish Provident. During our interview he confirmed he was a non-smoker. We checked and double-checked and confirmed with him he did not smoke. Interestingly back then in those days cigars were permitted – and underwriters did not count them as 'smoking' and he confirmed clearly he did not smoke, and we recorded this in our notes.

It took us one week to process the life policy. It took the bank around five months, but as he said, "I am saving £40 per month until it goes on risk." This demonstrated a lack of knowledge or simple reasoning on the part of the client, the effect of bullying and intimidation by their bank and a level of incompetence and commitment on the part of the directors of the bank/insurance company and their slovenly administration, poor level of commitment, and lack of client care.

After about 18 months he called me to confirm he had been to the doctor who had diagnosed him with melanoma cancer and he could not pay the premiums. We informed him his policy covered critical illness and waiver of premium which was covered in his policy with us. I also confirmed his bank policy also covered the illness, as we conducted a comparison from the outset. We told him to submit his claim through his bank. We informed him he would need to attend a medical, which he did and the melanoma cancer was confirmed. During the medical the doctor asked him if he smoked, he said no and then said, "Well maybe just one at Christmas." The doctor correctly wrote down the statement and sent it to the insurance companies. Both companies declined to pay out because he had claimed to be a non-smoker, on the basis of 'non-disclosure' rules. The insurance company took the decision based on the information now presented that he had not been honest when making the declaration on the application form – which they were fully entitled to do.

I contacted Scottish Provident and confirmed his details: a young businessman, wife, two young daughters, small business owner, self-employed and a large bank overdraft. I also pointed out the situation with the bank, and his decision to go with Scottish Provident, and the reduction in the bank assurance. I also pointed out and was able to demonstrate my questions, and my highlighting the 'No Smoking' declaration recorded on my agenda, and contemporaneous notes recorded the fact I had explained the criteria: no smoking for three years.

We sent this off to Scottish Provident who looked at the claim, the background, and given the circumstances from the doctor's records, background reports and our records and the amount of information we had taken, and the thoroughness of our process, the claims department agreed to review and reassess the claim. After one week they came back to me and offered £189,000. The reason for their reviewed decision was that they had looked at the entire background, i.e. his reason for requesting life assurance and critical illness, and had taken the view to look more appropriately on the claim – and paid out. The claims department took a view and had subsequently taken the life assurance rates for a smoker back to the commencement of the contract and calculated the amount of life assurance he could have had at that time and offered to pay out that amount as being a fair and reasonable decision.

He paid off the overdraft, brought mortgage payments up to date and brought his life back together, thanks to Scottish Provident and their attention to detail and, most importantly, their claims handling.

Now that is what I call protection. He accepted the offer from Scottish Provident and it was paid into his bank account within seven days of accepting the offer. The money was paid into his bank where he had filed his other claim for the life assurance and critical illness that he had been intimidated and bullied into taking out through the bank. Fourteen months later he was eventually offered £39,000 in full and final settlement from his bank who had sold him this poor quality protection, under pressure and bullying by the bank as a client, and as a result of his bank overdraft – which the bank wanted protected, and which he had accepted. Poor claims settlement is one of the most dangerous hazards when looking at any company offering a life assurance policy.

But protecting against a catastrophe is not just about protecting against premature death.

Sometimes you have to provide protection for living too long! We are all living longer now as a result of advances in medical science and mortality rates for men and women are increasing steadily. From retirement at the current age of 60, it can mean a further 30 years or more in retirement. Maintaining your desired lifestyle through retirement is now becoming even more important.

Those who purchase products for investments can lose much of their investments because they have not selected the correct product or considered the correct asset allocation or looked at the risks involved. Money invested in the stock market is a market which is volatile and which has inherent risks, which means your capital invested can go up or down and you may not get back your original investment. People invest in the stock market for various reasons. Some invest because they are greedy, or have the expectations for great returns. The markets are littered with people who have invested at the height of the markets, i.e. at the highest cost, and sell when markets drop and consolidate losses. Even seasoned investment managers cannot time the market. Their big advantage is they are in the market for the long term, looking after clients' money.

Newspapers and money magazines report funds that have done well as a matter of marketing, to attract new money. These newspaper reporters very seldom dig down into the structure of the fund, or the assets it contains, or the reason behind its success. These are the headline grabbers – for sales and marketing of the investment house or insurance company, firstly for the magazine to attract new readers, and secondly to attract new investors to the fund.

When a fund or share has increased in value is it likely the share will increase as much in the future, as it has already seen its share price or unit price grow significantly? Unless there is a special reason, the share price may not have the growth opportunity it had in the past. If a share or fund price has increased in value quickly, there is a reason behind it. You need to assess, and make a thorough investigation to assess the reason behind the price rise and assess if it is likely to rise in value again? If so, by how much? Or has it peaked?

Many people refer to these reports and price rises as 'if it is in the paper, it is in the price'. You need to judge if you are now buying this unit or share at the top of the market or near the top of the market, and question, what is the chance it will grow as much in value again? What period of time will you need to give it to find future price increases? What needs to happen to make the price rise again?

As part of a financial plan any losses can be looked at to offset against other profits to reduce tax, but in the stock market it is often the case where fear replaces greed for investment returns when markets drop in value. As a consequence, shares or units are sold. One reason for this is lack of fundamentals, or checks on assets in the fund, charges, the investment manager or investment group. Put simply, a lack of understanding of what an individual has purchased. When a fund or share has increased in value there may be no good reason for its purchase other than it was in the paper as a tip.

In my opinion, an individual should look at their portfolio regularly, take profits and bank them. I firmly believe portfolio checks should be consistent to see if rebalancing is in order to maintain the correct asset allocation. An individual should look at losses, check the reason behind the losses, and where necessary sell.

Selecting the correct asset allocation for an investment portfolio should be uppermost prior to making an investment of any kind. Tax applied to these and the charges must be taken into account and should form part of the strategy.

It is not possible within the scope of this book to deal with the six stages of life from birth, school and university, starting work, having a family and into retirement before looking to make the most of investments to provide additional income in retirement. It is important to recognise that the different stages of life have different needs. Early in life, when starting out with little or no money, life assurance should form a reasonable part of your needs. Purchase of the correct protection policies as early as possible can be most profitable later in life. As life progresses, and marriage and families come along, protection becomes even more important and forms a major need. However, often two salaries are reduced to one as children and the requirement for educational costs come to the fore. As one partner stays at home as housewife or house husband, the loss of their salary could provide a major financial shortfall where no protection is in place. The cost of caring for the family home and the family by a housewife/husband who can work up to 50 hours a week can be very expensive. Once people get to their late thirties and early forties costs increase and it is harder to keep saving regularly.

One of the most important aspects of living is to start saving up to 10% of salaries in the most tax-efficient manner – and for the long term. This strategy means you are saving for additional income in retirement. Usually a commission-based adviser will look to sell a pension plan but these contracts, whilst tax efficient, have restrictions. The longer the term you have to invest, the higher the level of risk you can take for the opportunity of higher returns. Investing in a pension plan can also provide for protection in later life, e.g. if the pension plan holder dies the fund can be taken by the spouse, or if written in trust or a nomination it may be passed down to children.

Unfortunately, a pension plan requires some 30 years of premiums and investment before the fund grows and reaches any significant amount. A good long-term life assurance policy can protect during the interim until the pension plan grows. The State Pension Age (SPA) is currently 65 for men. For women it is to be gradually increased from 60 to 65 over the 10 years to April 2020, the objective being to equalise the SPA from 2024 to 2046, and it is to be gradually increased from 65 to 68 years.

The basic State Pension is a flat rate pension that is payable to any individual who has sufficient 'qualifying years'. Under changes made from 6 April 2010 by the Pensions Act 2007, the number of qualifying years needed for a full basic State Pension is 30 for both men and women. Individuals without sufficient qualifying years (either from earnings or credits) receive a proportion of the full amount.

State Earnings Related Pensions (SERPS) accrued between 1978 and 2002 is paid in addition to the basic State Pension. When it was replaced in 2002, SERPS was targeting a pension of approximately 20% of the employee's middle band earnings i.e. earnings between the lower and upper earnings limits at SPA.

The State Second Pension (S2P) came into effect on 6 April 2002 and is currently an earnings-related scheme like SERPS which it replaced.

Further changes to pensions legislation means the government is introducing a flat rate pension set at some £155 per week. The government is removing some of the requirements and criteria, but there does not appear to be any proper financial accounting, or funding in place by the government, which means you should take more control of your own finances and savings regime.

On top of this the government has introduced auto enrolment for work-related pension schemes from October 2012 which is arranged through your employer, and can include cleaners and carers etc. These transitional arrangements put the responsibility and cost on the employer, and requires the employees to invest.

The initial contribution is 1% from employers and 1% from the employee – to be taken directly from salary. This is to increase in October 2018 (i.e. 2018/2019 tax year) to 3% from employer and 4% from employees (taken directly from your salary) along with the proposed current, 'government incentive of 1%'. This means a total of 8% going into auto enrolment pension arrangements.

The earnings trigger for auto enrolment is £10,000 and the qualifying earnings band is £5,824 up to £42,385. The legislation provides for increases, and may follow along the lines of the Australian government pension scheme arrangement.

Having regard to the various State Pensions it is essential that you prioritise your long-term retirement planning to ensure you can continue with the lifestyle that you desire.

Planning for retirement should be one of the highest priorities. This should be the cornerstone of your long-term investment strategy. However, a pension plan product should form only a part of your retirement planning but not the only investment. Investments in venture capital trusts offer 30% tax relief, tax-free income and opportunities for growth and access to the full fund. Enterprise investment schemes offer the opportunity for tax relief and investment returns. Individual savings plans, unit trusts and insurance bonds also offer tax-free income (up to 5% tax free as it is classed as return of capital).

Planning for retirement should be the second highest priority after protection. Planning for additional income in retirement takes many forms and should consist of several asset-backed investments which can provide returns above inflation over the long term.

As you go through life there are many demands on your money: house, mortgage, car, children and keeping up a lifestyle which is attainable and achievable. Unfortunately, many people adopt the 'live for the present and worry about the future at some later stage' approach. Leaving retirement planning to later life is expensive and inefficient. But retirement can be planned for and built into your lifetime cash flow model.

The life/work balance

The objective is to build up wealth, regularly, over the long term to enable you to sustain your lifestyle throughout retirement. You will need to consider what you wish to achieve and what you want to do in retirement – and with more time on your hands you will probably be busier in retirement than you were when you were working.

The benefits of pound cost averaging

Should you decide to invest a lump sum in a share, you buy the share at today's price and sell the share in a year's time at the market price at that time. During the year the share price may go up or down and by contributing regularly on a monthly basis you purchase the shares at the monthly price. This could mean that by contributing monthly you might expect to obtain more shares by the end of the year due to the fluctuating share price.

However, it is worth remembering that if you have conducted good solid research you might wish to purchase the share at today's price by way of a lump sum and be optimistic the share price will increase.

Investing regularly obtains the benefits of pound cost averaging, and by adopting a regular savings and investing pattern, the money spent will not be noticed quite so much unless you have selected an unachievable amount. The amount chosen must be affordable. The longer the term, the higher the risk you may take for the opportunity of higher returns. However, you need to discuss this with your financial adviser.

For example, many people enjoy sports and sports club membership, for example of their golf club, tennis club, or bowls club. These clubs arrange functions and society outings, and matches for the benefit of members, and participating in these brings further costs. Planning these costs in advance can take the strain out of finding money each year for membership. Failure to look at these costs early enough, or at all, could result in having to look at your finances and compromising the benefits of membership, e.g. switching from a seven-day membership to a five-day or restricted membership, which involves a change of lifestyle and rearranging your time, and the complications to meet these restrictions.

A simple investment made sooner rather than later can address these costs early and, having identified them all and used your assumed rate of inflation, you are in the position to develop your strategy and build it into your Lifesmart® lifestyle strategy. You can be prepared!

This Lifesmart® strategy can be used with most situations where you have regular and increasing costs from sports club memberships to timeshare maintenance fees. Holiday costs, buildings and contents, and gas and electricity costs can be similarly identified and costs accounted for. The Lifesmart® Financial Plan identifies each of these costs and helps you identify your requirements, set your strategy and deal with your income and your expenditure throughout your life.

Planning

Planning is all about being prepared. Being organised, being ahead of the game. By adopting this strategy, you will become proactive rather than reactive. You will be in control.

By planning your expenditure accurately you will see where you are overspending or not spending enough. You will be prepared to have your funds ready for your holiday, and rather than make use of credit cards and pay high levels of interest, these savings will be held in your account.

Each year you should conduct a year end portfolio check. Look at your portfolio and check the asset allocation, and where required see if a rebalancing would be in order. Look at your portfolio to scout around for losers, and where appropriate sell them. Make use of the capital gains allowance.

Take profits from your winners, and bank them. Trimming profits is a good habit to acquire.

Maximise your tax-efficient investments in NISAs and maximise your retirement fund pension contributions. In the current year the maximum allowable contributions to your self-invested Personal Pension (SIPP) is £40,000 or 100% of your annual salary (up to £40,000 gross) and with basic rate tax deducted, this means you may contribute a maximum of £32,000 and basic rate tax is added, so the total investment is £40,000 maximum. Any higher rate tax is reclaimed through your self-assessment. You may also look to the input periods and go back over three years to maximise your pension contributions.

Look at other tax-efficient investments and where appropriate build up their portfolios.

Regular premiums or investing benefit from pound cost averaging which is much better than the scattergun approach of lump sums paid at indiscriminate times. Regularise and regulate your investments, build your portfolios for the future. Bring good solid commitment to your savings and investments.

CHAPTER 12:
Keep your finances independent

The reason for financial planning is to take control of your destiny, first and foremost. Gather all the relevant information, decide what you want to achieve – and make it happen.

Once you have decided on your objective(s), develop your lifetime cash flow plan, review all the information, build in your assumptions and decide on your strategy. For your financial planning I would recommend you use a trusted adviser who can demonstrate they are independent, free from bias and can look into your financial planning and strategy in depth, with knowledge, skill and expertise, and will provide you with a second opinion. An independent source removing the emotion, and expressing a transparent structure and checking and re-checking for accuracy and the detail, and checking how each change affects the rest of your plan. A good financial plan has to balance, change, and react when necessary. A good planner gives a good second opinion using their own knowledge, skill and experience. This is of major benefit to your finances.

Many people aspire to achieve, whether in wealth or to meet their personal ambitions or in their chosen career or business.

We look at each client individually, and assess their needs and their requirements in life, nearing retirement and in retirement. More and more people have different hobbies. Most couples now have two cars. Each individual has different requirements to see the family, or perhaps they have moved away, or more commonly nowadays gone abroad. For those in their late thirties or early forties, you need to plan it now, not put it off.

I had a lovely meeting with a rather gruff old regimental colonel, of the old school, who had been particularly successful throughout his army career and through retirement. He had been moved around the world and enjoyed many challenges – and if the army teaches you anything it is how to manage people. Nowadays he enjoyed a regular game of golf at his prestigious golf club and attending many army functions and other more local occasions. His wife enjoyed going to see their grandchildren, was immersed in the rural community and helped to organise many local and charitable events. The colonel's pride and joy was a rather large, powerful, sleek Jaguar which cost a lot to buy before he retired, cost a lot to run and cost a lot of money to insure. His wife had a 1.4 Renault Clio. We looked into the costs of each car and built these into the Lifesmart® cash flow model. During our conversation the colonel quipped, "Of course when I retire we will not need to run two cars." His wife's face sank visibly; you could feel the tension in the air as she could see her lovely pride and joy disappear, her Renault Clio, and her freedom slipping away.

To discover more and delve deeper into his response, and that of his wife, I turned to the colonel and made the point by asking, "So could you do without the Jag then?" There was a long pause as my words sank in, his face dropped and he looked aghast. Obviously he was only thinking of the Renault because that did not affect his freedom, but had not considered his wife's position. His wife on the other hand was visibly relieved. He was even more shaken when I said, "Would you really enjoy becoming a taxi service again?" As a long silent pause ensued, I reminded him of the years of being a taxi for his children to school, to sports, piano lessons, and back and forth from night clubs or parties or charitable events. It was his good idea to buy a second car to devolve some of the responsibility to his wife in the first place. I also asked if he would enjoy driving his wife to and from the supermarket for the shopping, dropping her off to see the children and grandchildren, staying or returning to collect her. Dropping her off for the Women's Institute and then asking his wife to drive him to the golf club in his 4.2 litre Jaguar?

I then suggested when he looked at his personal situation in depth, selling the Renault Clio was not really an option. The reality was they led separate lives and they both needed a car so they could be independent. Whilst costs were an issue, they were necessary costs to retain their quality of life and freedom for each other and that really two cars *were* necessary. It was brought home when we went into it further and discovered the daughter often came over and drove the mother around and they spent time shopping together. Somehow I don't think the colonel would have been so keen to see his daughter disappearing to the shops with her mother in his beloved Jaguar.

That was their life – that was the lifestyle that they really wanted, and needed to continue. We built the costs into the financial plan, made assumptions on increasing costs in years to come and we made provision to purchase new cars in five years' time, if they wished. With the cost of fuel reducing by around 55% they had spare income. They don't need it so we have placed it in their Wild Living Fund. Everyone should have a Wild Living Fund

Nowadays however, with the increasing number of marriage breakdowns, civil partnerships and partnerships breaking down, we live in an age where life has become very complex. Building wealth and finance into these new family structures becomes more complicated and we find the growth in partnership breakdowns becoming such a burden that the Law Society has introduced a new system called Collaborative Law to help those who need legal assistance, by way of collaboration rather than expensive court cases. Collaborative Law is a facility to deal with their situation, through discussion and compromise, without the complications and expense of using two sets of solicitors, courts and court costs, recriminations and the large inherent cost of legal advice.

Collaborative Law is not a simple solution for a quick or easy get out, it is a simplified system which requires much in-depth discussion and a reality check allowing common sense and compromise in a structured environment. It can still be seriously expensive.

Before you plan your lifestyle or your finances, you need to draft a valid Will. The importance of a Will as your starting point in your personal financial planning cannot be overvalued. The Will is a most important tool to provide succession planning for your finances – or for succession planning for your business.

Before you plan your desired lifestyle or your finances your Will identifies your beneficiaries, your nominations and those you wish to inherit and in what amounts. Your Will should be drafted to take account of your estate and to pass your assets in a tax efficient manner to those who you wish to benefit. Your Will should include facilities to reduce any potential Inheritance Tax on your estate and benefit your beneficiaries in an effective way.

For example, when you start out in life and money is tight it is quite simple to create a significant pot of money for your children by setting up a life assurance policy in trust which will become effective on your death releasing an amount of money free of Inheritance Tax in the current tax regime. These policies should be set up on a singular basis and whilst this is usually slightly more expensive, it means death benefit is paid out on first death, more efficiently, rather than waiting for the second partner to die. Secondly, the second partner will retain their protection when the first partner dies. Joint life first death policies mean the surviving partner loses their protection. This is usually when they are significantly older and therefore are more expensive to replace. Health issues as you grow older may mean increased premiums due to ill health.

Similarly with investing, each partner should assess their own attitude to risk. Each individual will have a slightly different attitude to the level of risk they wish to adopt as a result of their age, the number of years they wish to invest and/or their own view on the market and trust in the financial institutions. Advisers usually choose equity-linked investments because they are remunerated by way of commissions, normally by way of a percentage, e.g. 1.5% of a portfolio for their remuneration. This is unclear and not transparent. It is often taken from your tax-efficient investments, e.g. NISA pension funds, and creates a drag on the investment which affects your total return.

In 2016 the Financial Conduct Authority (FCA) is to remove commissions, and an adviser's status and their services and fees should be clearly stated and in financial terms. Many banks and tied agents choose 'managed funds' as their default fund rather than make an accurate assessment of the correct level of risk for each individual and design a portfolio of assets on an individual basis.

Now, with the advances in technology there is the opportunity for 'Robo Advice', a facility where investment portfolios are designed by a provider where you can have access to a portfolio which meets your risk profile. These are often cheaper than an authorised adviser, due to the fact you take responsibility for the choice of investment in these funds. Other opportunities exist with index trackers which track a specific index or indices. These low-cost facilities are now widely available, and relatively inexpensive.

Whilst planning is important, assessing the correct asset allocation is fundamental to building a portfolio and portfolio planning. Having the correct asset classes within the portfolio means you can increase your wealth without chopping and changing your holdings and losing out to the barrage of ongoing charges and consolidation of your losses. This is where a good quality professional authorised adviser can really add value. Employing properly qualified professionals to assess your asset allocation is fundamental. This is opposed to advisers who are 'fund pickers', usually in an inconsistent way, using flavour of the month funds.

The research behind products and funds is a vital ingredient, and expensive. The benefit is good quality in-depth research of assets which are appropriate and complement each other to diversify your holdings in order to meet your desired outcomes.

When you lose money in an investment it requires a higher level of interest to bring your investment back to the point prior to where it went down. For example, if your investment of £30,000 drops by 10% i.e. £3,000 to £27,000, a growth of 10% on £27,000 will only increase the £27,000 to £29,700. It will require a growth of 11.112 % to bring the investment of £27,000 back to £30,000 (and a few pennies i.e. £30,000.24). The higher the losses, the more interest growth you require to bring your investment back to the price before the drop. Serious decisions need to be taken if there are significant drops in the stock market investments, and decisions taken as to whether it is more beneficial to leave them to recover or sell and reinvest elsewhere (taking into account new upfront charges for setting up and buying and selling).

Changes to the requirement of individuals then is crucial when deciding on which assets to invest into. Risk factors play an even more crucial role. Understanding risk is essential when assessing a portfolio and the required return for the amount of risk taken. Each individual has a level of risk they are willing to take, and this must be assessed separately.

By adopting a strategy to retain control of your finances independently, you can plan to reduce each partner's or individual's tax. You can obtain more tax relief on investments, for example pensions. More of the investment can be used to direct towards a partner who is a higher rate taxpayer whilst deposit accounts can be held in the lower rate taxpayer's name – once again reducing tax.

Understanding risk

Life is about compromise, life is about trade-off. Part of Lifesmart® financial planning strategy is discussing the various opportunities, compromise and about the trade-off. The trade-off may be about work versus family time. The trade-off on risk is to decide on the level of risk you are willing to take and your capacity for loss. The trade-off on risk to investments is around your expectations and your objective to obtain the return you need.

When you understand how an asset works or the companies within the investment, you increase your knowledge, you gain more confidence – and you should learn not to panic. When you know what you want to achieve you will be able to look at compromise and make better decisions.

With investment risk there are two basic risks investors face:

- First, the risk of losing money

- Second, the fear and lack of confidence

Risk of losing money over the short term. Over the shorter term – weeks, months and even a few years – the risk of losing money in volatile markets, featured in the newspapers and on television down to day traders and speculators. By adopting a good well-diversified portfolio, you reduce these risks dramatically. The stock market is awash with accumulators and speculators involved with regular trading trying to make a 'turn' as in market movements – daily, weekly or monthly. Many stock market investors attempt to emulate these 'stock pickers' but fail to recognise their knowledge, skills in gambling and their capacity for loss.

Many people count their losses quicker than look to their actual investment returns over their entire portfolio, or regularly monitor their portfolio and look at the reasons behind any growth or fall in value. Investors invariably focus on their losses in type of risk.

Risk comes in many guises and can be good. I believe volatility is good for investors – but you should not let it get in the way of your objectives. Using pound cost averaging and saving and investing regularly you can secure the benefits and reduce the volatility of your portfolio. By purchasing regularly into the asset-backed investments such as equities, or pooled investments such as unit trusts or investment trusts, you buy into the asset or unit each month as the unit price fluctuates. When unit prices are down you buy more units and as markets increase in value the unit price grows, and because you have purchased more units this is reflected in your portfolio value.

There are a number of risks you need to consider before investing. It is important to take emotion out of the decision. Risk and reward go hand in hand and you should reduce risk where possible when looking for a result.

> Similarly with investing, commission such as 3% to 4.5% upfront and a further 1% to 2% per annum for ongoing fees, taken from your tax efficient investments e.g. pensions funds or NISA's acts as a 'drag' on your portfolio. In my opinion it is better to pay fees direct, to analyse and reflect on the real 'value for money'. This provides clear, transparent and open and honest dealing, from your adviser.

> This is opposed to 'fund pickers', or being influenced by an inducement or some other form of sales pitch, without conducting any proper analysis or due diligence.

Market risk

Market risk comes with the exposure you have to a particular asset class (e.g. property, gilts or fixed income) or a sector such as equities, e.g. technology stocks or pharmaceuticals. It is the threat of the entire market losing money or selling when the markets drop such as in 2008/2009. You can limit market risk by diversifying into various markets. Many people buy their own residential property, have a mortgage and the property investment is the largest asset class, which makes an imbalance of asset classes.

Company specific risks

Operating risk and price risk are two factors which contribute to short-term volatility. Profits earnings or drops can entice the market makers to sell. Price risk has more to do with a company's stock than its business, and astute investors assess how expensive the stock is compared with the company's earnings cash flow or sales.

Economic risks

The world markets may act and react in many ways, and directly affect your portfolio. Diversification can assist to reduce the risks, but it is important to keep a check on markets and be fully involved. Any good fund manager has at their disposal an economic specialist internally or externally, e.g. Stephanie Flanders, Roger Bootle, Robert Peston and many more along with their in-depth research.

Country risks

Each country carries a further risk and the economics of each country and their prospects for growth are the attraction to fund managers, along with the risks attached.

It is important to look at the assets which you wish to include in your portfolio by selecting the level of growth you wish or the income. By selecting the geographical strategy, you can diversify your investments across some or all of the world. Deciding on your level of exposure to each country and the type of companies within each country you wish to be exposed to, e.g. large or small or the extent of the fund you wish to choose.

With all the markets in the world we only gather a very small level of information on investments. By adopting a system of funnelling down to your requirements, you will remove many of the poor quality investments. By selecting your geographical area asset allocation you can reduce the volatility further. Checking for overlap in your portfolios means greater diversification and reduces volatility.

Looking at your options in large companies or medium-sized companies and smaller companies, you can further increase your diversification. When checking your diversification, make sure you are not overly diversified as this will act as a drag on your investment returns.

By adopting a strategy of deciding what you wish to achieve and being proactive means you will be ahead of the game. The predator salesperson has to meet your criteria – not theirs.

Now that is what I call a plan!

As markets and economics change, be ready to adapt, adopt and improve.

Happy Financial Planning!

GLOSSARY

Arbitrage

A financial transaction which generates risk-free profit.

Beta

A measure of market risk.

Credit Risk

The risk that a counterparty may not meet its obligations.

Custodian

A financial institution which holds securities on behalf of investors.

Default Risk

See credit risk.

Exposure

Being affected by a source of risk.

Insurance Bonds

A life assurance policy, where the investor pays a lump sum whereby they can withdraw up to 5% of the original investment free of tax (this is classed as 'return of capital'). The capital gain is called a chargeable event and is added to your income.

Leverage

The combination and compounding of financial risks.

Liquidity Risk

The risk associated with the inability to raise cash.

New Individual Savings Plans (NISA)

A tax wrapper, up to the maximum amount which may be invested in cash, pooled investments or stocks and shares. Each financial institution decides which form of assets they will accept.

Personal Pension (SIPP)

A tax wrapper with specific tax advantages such as tax at basic rate is added to your contribution and any higher rate tax is reclaimed through your annual tax return. A tax-free lump sum may be taken from your pension fund of up to 25% of the fund value.

Portfolio

The combination of one or many financial instruments for investment purposes, made up of different asset classes, e.g. cash, gilts and fixed interest, property and equities. These can be broken down further into property (commercial industrial offices and residential) and equities UK and global, and segregated further into large companies for growth or income or medium-sized companies or smaller companies for growth or income.

Pound Cost Averaging

Pound cost averaging is best described as the technique of choosing to make your investments on a regular basis and averaging out the cost of your total investment over time. If you invest the same amount of money each month and the share price is down you get more for your money than when the share price is rising.

Risk

The exposure to an uncertainty.

Total Return

The total return on a portfolio of investments takes into account not only the capital appreciation on the portfolio but also the income received on the portfolio. The income typically consists of interest, dividends, and securities lending fees. Total return also takes into account charges against the portfolio and advisers' and product providers' charges.

$$\text{Total Return} = \frac{(P_1 - P_0) + D}{P_0}$$

Where P1 is initial price (to include increments less charges and fees)
P0 is end price
D is dividends

Unit Trusts

A unit trust is a pooled investment, normally with a designated fund manager and a team of experts who carry out research on the assets they may be intending to purchase.

Venture Capital Trusts (VCTs)

A more risky lump sum investment where you may obtain up to 30% tax relief on investments up to £200,000. These contracts are set out over a period of five years. Dividends may be paid out tax free.

ABOUT THE AUTHOR

Born in Selkirk, Ian has over 30 years' experience in various roles in the finance industry including at Hambro Life, Scottish Widows and the BMA Services Ltd as an IFA before deciding to open his own practice in 1997 to provide sound advice and to help people get their finances in order. Ian enjoys working with people and helping them to  build their wealth in the most efficient and effective manner so that they can enjoy their desired lifestyle up to and throughout retirement.

After leaving university, Ian was determined to fulfil his dream of becoming a trusted salesman. With complete training from prospecting through technical issues to the end sale, and working hands on in each of these areas of finance, he became a very successful agent in each of the companies he worked.

To fulfil his passion, Ian delivers workshops and boardroom seminars in many of these areas to help people better understand their money, how it works, and how to make it work more efficiently, more effectively and the rewards and personal benefits these can bring.

While living in Fife, Ian joined Round Table and has remained an involved member until joining 41 Club having reached the age of 45!

He is also involved in a number of different charities and is currently a trustee on the Board of the Cambridge Sea Cadets.

Ian is a qualified BASI ski instructor as well as an assistant white water canoe instructor in Division 1 Scottish white water championships and he also trained and completed a parachute jump for the Royal National Institute for the Blind ... whilst retaining his fear of heights!

Ian is a fee-based Financial Planning Consultant and the Managing Director of LifeSmart® Financial Planning Ltd and Westminster Wills Ltd.

Contact Ian at:

ian@westminsterwills.co.uk

www.westminsterwills.co.uk

Telephone: +44 (0)1727 867888 / +44 (0)1727 833857

Lightning Source UK Ltd.
Milton Keynes UK
UKOW06f1024130416

272154UK00001B/2/P